ELIZABETHAN DEDICATIONS AND PREFACES

George Gascoigne Presenting *The Tale of Hemetes The Heremyte* to the Queen, January 1, 1576

AN ANTHOLOGY OF

Elizabethan Dedications

Prefaces

Edited by

CLARA GEBERT

Philadelphia

UNIVERSITY OF PENNSYLVANIA PRESS

MCMXXXIII

Manufactured in the United States of America

LONDON
HUMPHREY MILFORD
OXFORD UNIVERSITY PRESS

TO MY FATHER

PREFACE

AS first editions form in most instances the original source to which all questions of text must be referred, first editions, either in original or in photostat or in facsimile form, have been used in the preparation of this text. In a few cases when the book was not printed until the eighteenth century, manuscript copies have been employed. The date assigned a title is not necessarily the date of its first appearance in print, but the date at which that particular dedication or preface was composed. In most cases the two dates coincide; but there are a few discrepancies, as in the case of *Gorboduc* and *The Faerie Queene*. As far as possible, the punctuation of the early editions and manuscripts has been retained. Likewise, in spelling, only those changes were made which were absolutely necessary. The long *ſ* has become s, where necessary v has been changed to u, i to j, j to y, and y to i. All contractions have been expanded to their full value throughout. An attempt has been made in the format of the volume to suggest as much of the typographic flavor of the original dedications as is consistent with the requirements of uniformity.

In endeavoring to secure these early editions, many obligations have been incurred. To Dr. A. S. W. Rosenbach, who graciously opened his Philadelphia and New York treasures to me, I am especially indebted. I am grateful, for aid in locating some of the rare and unique manuscripts, to Mr. Cecil K. Edmonds of the Henry E. Huntington Library. I wish to acknowledge my indebtedness to the following libraries: The Henry E. Huntington Library, Folger Library, Harvard University Library, University of Chicago Library, New York Public Library, Philadelphia Free Library, Library Company of Philadelphia, Library of Congress, Bodleian Library, Emanuel College Library, British Museum Library, the Dyce library of the Victoria and Albert Museum, and the library of the Duke of Devonshire, all of which have enabled me to secure the text in this volume. To the library of the University of Pennsylvania, including the Furness Library, I am appreciative not so much for first editions as for the large Elizabethan library in English literature and in the various departments in which I did my reading prior to making the selections.

The deepest debt of gratitude, however, I owe to Professor Felix E. Schelling, who suggested the subject and who has been most sympathetic and helpful. Only those who have been present in his classroom, and only those who have worked intimately with him can realize how difficult it is to say merely "thank you." We thank one for personal gifts and favors, but before a touch of the "gleam" we humbly bow and pray that we may pass but a little along.

Clara L. Gebert.

Philadelphia, 1933.

CONTENTS

INTRODUCTION

INTRODUCTION

ANTHOLOGIES of English writings begin at least with *The Mirror for Magistrates,* and their variety in kind and feature can be no new thing. Famous are the poetical anthologies of Elizabethan times from *Tottel's Miscellany* to Davison's *Poeticall Rhapsody;* and even anthologies of quotations such as *England's Helicon* and Bodenham's *Belvedere, or the Garden of the Muses* flourished in their day. It is the purpose of this book to gather a collection of dedications and prefaces to books written within what is usually called the Elizabethan period, less for the mere novelty of such a gathering than for the light which these expressions of contemporary mood and fashion cannot but throw upon the authors, the publishers, and the patrons of Elizabethan books. While there are of course examples of verse employed to dedicatory purposes, by far the greatest number of examples of this feature in our older English books are cast in prose and, as was but natural, the epistolary is quite the usual form. Last to be written but first in place, the prefatory epistle usually sets forth the aim and purpose of the book, and the circumstances that inspired it, thus letting us into a closer association alike with the author and often with the text itself.

In the preparation of the following collection many more books have been examined and analyzed for the purpose than those which have been accepted. And while it would be idle to suggest that the search has been completely exhaustive, it may not be too much to say that it has included most of the important books in literary history within the period in question and may thus be considered sufficiently exhaustive to be representative. From the mass of material examined a hundred titles have been selected for their historic value, intrinsic interest, inherent charm or style, information not found elsewhere, or simply because they are typical. Such a selection must necessarily be subjective despite all endeavors to the contrary; yet it is hoped that what has ultimately been chosen may justify itself to such extent as to represent a nucleus of Elizabethan thought and fashion within the very considerable range which these books represent.

The limitations of an anthology such as this are at once obvious. Even though the term "Elizabethan" is construed liberally to cover the reigns of both Queen Elizabeth and King James, certain dates must be set to establish the termini. For this purpose, the years 1557 and 1623 have been chosen. The first is the date of the earliest publication of that epoch-making book, *Tottel's Miscellany,* the earliest collection of modern lyrical verse; the second, the date of the appearance of the first folio of Shakespeare's plays. In addition to limitations superimposed by date, length must also be a determining factor. William Harrison's *Description of England,* intended as a preface to Holinshed's *Chronicles of England, Scotland, and Ireland,* runs to 250 pages even in the old folio edition; and Fulke Greville's *Life of Sidney,* planned as a dedication to his *Works,* sums up an entire volume. Then there are other important prefaces, treatises in their own right, which must be similarly, however reluctantly, excluded. Among these are Dr. John Dee's mathematical preface to *Euclid's Elements of Geometry,* 1570, a text clear, concise, well organized, awe inspiring, however now obsolete, containing also the interesting "digression apologetical" against accusations of necromancy, and incidentally divulging Dee's poverty and sacrifices to the cause of learning. Among lengthy prefaces in the field of literary criticism are E.K.'s epistle to Gabriel Harvey preceding Spenser's *Shepheards Calendar,* 1579, a defense of Spenser's archaic language; Thomas Nashe's preface to Robert Greene's *Menaphon,* 1589, abounding in interesting contemporary references; Sir John Harington's *Apologie of Poetrie* prefixed to his famous translation of *Orlando Furioso,* 1591, expounding again the principles laid down in Sidney's *Apologie for Poetry;* and George Chapman's theories of translation and his defense of Homer, preceding his translation of the *Iliad,* 1598–1611, and the *Odyssey,* 1614. Spenser's letter to Sir Walter Raleigh explaining carefully the allegory of the *Faerie Queene,* 1590–1596, for fear of misinterpretation by censors; Sir Walter Raleigh's philosophic and expository preface to the *History of the World,* 1614, written while in prison; Sir Francis Bacon's learned prefaces to the *Novum Organum,* 1620; Robert Burton's minute analysis, outlines, and personal problems in his satirical preface to the *Anatomy of Melancholy,* 1621, one of the most interesting parts of the book—all of these must also be most regretfully omitted, for this group of prefaces by itself would constitute no small volume. Again, in order to keep this book within reasonable bounds, only seldom have both dedication and epistle to the reader of the same title been reproduced. Another restriction concerns form. From what has already been said, it is evident that dedicatory sonnets and allied verse forms are debarred. The dedicatory sonnet first comes into notice about 1590, and it rapidly gained in popularity, at first supplementing and in time often supplanting the prose dedicatory epistle. Should anyone wonder why the circumstance that neither Joshua Sylvester nor Sir John

Davies, for instance, is represented in this collection, it is because their dedications and prefaces are wholly in verse.

Limitations of date, length, and form leave us, then, with a collection of prose dedications and epistles to the reader, chosen from Elizabethan books between 1557 and 1623 that are not too long to be reproduced in their entirety. The arrangement is strictly chronological in the order of the first appearance of each in print; for it is believed that the historic development of this form of writing may thus best be traced.

Considering the variety of tone, occasion, purpose, and material in question with which these epistles are concerned, an enumeration of some of these characteristics, if not a classification or distinction of the material, may not seem out of place. There is for example a large group which is expository in character, stating the sources, aim, or plan: in this collection represented by Stow's *Summary of English Chronicles,* 1565, for instance. Justification for undertaking the work often becomes the ruling idea of an epistle as in Chettle's *Kind-Hartes Dreame,* 1592. The autobiographical preface is illustrated by *Greenes Groatsworth of Wit Bought with a Million of Repentance,* 1592, or Lodge's *A Margarite of America,* 1596. Besides communicating a close personal touch, this often furnishes authentic data not to be found elsewhere. There are prefaces again which are largely speculative or philosophical in character; R.G.'s *A Good Speed to Virginia,* 1609, for example, reveals the thoughts and ideals of the Elizabethan mind. Still again, some prefaces are planned to supply information: Such is Hakluyt's *Virginia Richly Valued,* 1609, describing the natural resources and natives of that colony; or to offer instruction, as Campion's *New Waye of Making Fowre Partes in Counterpoint,* 1610, the preface of which sets forth "a briefe

Method teaching to Sing." Such matter, though often obsolete, is likely to be of unusual historic interest. There is a large group of doctrinal prefaces, concerned with contemporary and ephemeral controversies among Romanists, Protestants, Puritans, critics or censors represented variously by Parsons, the Jesuit; Richard Hooker, the eminent divine; and Philip Stubbs, the Puritan reformer. The Martin Marprelate controversy with its mass of argument and vituperation belongs here as well as the prefaces to the reader in the numerous editions of the Bible omitted in this volume mainly because of their length and transitory interest. George Sandys, for instance, in the dedication to his *Travells,* 1615, perpetrates a veritable sermon, and Loe's *A Months Mind,* 1620, expresses equally if in another way the utterance of a devout nature and the difficulties of bringing such utterances to a discreet end. Still again there is an interesting species of the prefatory epistle which centers in a quarrel or where the author seeks notoriety or aims to spread his personal opinions. Such is the paper war in which Greene and Nashe were engaged against the Harvey brothers. This grew to such a common nuisance that it had to be stilled by the burning of the books of all concerned by the common hangman. This is exemplified in this collection by Nashe's proffer of reconciliation in his preface to *Christ's Teares Over Jerusalem,* 1593. Then there is the notable and long-continued attack on the stage illustrated by Gosson and Rainolds, with Lodge and Heywood on the side of refutation; and more internecine, the notorious "war of the theatres," Jonson versus Dekker and Marston, which by means of dramas more than epistles occupied the scene with its flashlight of dissension for a brief time. The books satirizing fashion, the plays and pamphlets in the arraignment or defense of women, as Swetnam's *The Arraignment of Lewd, Idle, Forward and Inconstant Women,* 1615, confuted by the anonymous satirical comedy, *Swetnam, the Woman Hater Arraigned by Women,* 1620, afford us again and again satirical prefaces not without interest or at least amusement today. Campion versus Daniel on rhyme, Vincent versus Brooke on heraldry, and Camden versus Brooke, Grafton versus Stow on history: all clamor for attention. Not infrequently the arguments within the confines of the book become so heated that they bubble over into the preface, where attacks are apt to become personal and where the ferment finds its veritable outlet.

To continue in our enumeration, literary criticism finds a fitting place in the preface, for there the author has his opportunity to discuss or defend the theories embodied in his book. Thus *Tottel's Miscellany,* 1557, offers a defense of poetry in general and of English poetry in particular; George Whetstone's *Promos and Cassandra,* 1578, treats dogmatically of the moral and didactic purpose of his story; and Giles Fletcher's *Licia,* 1593, discusses the nature of the vernacular. More personal is Nashe's analysis of his own style and language in his *Christ's Teares Over Jerusalem,* 1593; Chapman's disquisition on translation in his work on Homer's *Iliad,* 1598–1611, and Jonson's explanation of his method of working according to classic precepts in *Sejanus,* 1605. No excuse need be offered for including matter such as this in the collection, and these cases form but a small representation of the numberless apologies prefixed to Elizabethan books. To these dicta, theories, and criticisms of contemporary authors we may add one or two further examples. There is John Fletcher's definition of the pastoral and tragi-comedy in his epistle to *The Faith-*

ful Shepherdess, c. 1610, and Drayton's interesting little treatise on the ode in his preface to *Poemes, Lyrick and Pastorall, c.* 1606. Important passages involving the mention and criticism of contemporary authors are to be found in the epistle to *Greenes Groatsworth of Wit,* 1592, and Chettle's *Kind-Hartes Dreame,* 1592.

A final group may be distinguished, and that is the strange variety of epistle which seems written more or less to mystify the reader. During the author's absence from town, a friend has had his book published surreptitiously, or the author was forced to publish his book because so many copies, mean and defaced, had been sent abroad by dishonest printers. It seems impossible to determine to what extent the surreptitious printing of books, presumably intended only for manuscript publication, was common to the Elizabethan age. The printing of stolen playhouse copies, of actor's versions, or even of copies secured by stenography we recognize as common to the practices of the day. But the degree of the author's responsibility for this state of things in many examples must remain a matter of conjecture. An assumption of the age declared that a gentleman could not permit his name to appear in print and that to do so smacked vulgarly of trade and barter. It seems likely that this affectation of a genteel sensitiveness was responsible for much mystification. We know that Bacon's *Essayes,* 1597, hurried into a permitted printing because there had appeared a pirated edition. Gascoigne's epistles prefixed to *A Hundreth Sundrie Flowers,* 1572, are most likely a mere hoax to mystify readers in order to relieve the poet of responsibility for the publication of his own works. Just how much of this was premeditated and fabricated, or how much was mere accident and clumsiness, we leave our readers to judge from the epistles of this nature which follow. The mystifications and paradoxes of such prefaces and dedications are often very thin, and provocative in us of little more than an indulgent smile. In the cases of some very well-known works—such, for example, as *The Sonnets of Shakespeare,* as in *Avisa,* or *Love's Martyr* and some others—they leave us an insoluble literary or biographical problem.

This selection of dedications and prefaces is representative of certain features of change on the part of author, patron, printer, and public. During the Elizabethan era there was a gradual disintegration of the aristocratic system of private literary patronage and the beginning of economic independence on the part of authors.[1] The allegation that the birth of the "professional" author, one who gained a livelihood by selling his writings, took place during this period, is abundantly substantiated by this study of dedications and prefaces.

A dedicatory epistle is a formal inscription whereby the author releases his book to the world in general, but in the name of his dedicatee in particular. His long labor over, he bids his book adieu; and partly with love and hope, partly with hesitation and fear, he bequeaths it to at least one who will receive it kindly. The practice of dedicating books is of great antiquity, for patronage itself is an ancient institution. As Drayton well puts it, patronage "is seated by custome (from which wee are now bolde to assume authoritie) to beare the names of our friends upon the fronts of our bookes, as Gentlemen use to set their Armes over their gates. Some say this began by the *Heroes* and brave spirits of the old world, which were desirous to be thought to patronize

1 See Phoebe Sheavyn, *The Literary Profession in Elizabethan Age,* Manchester Univ. Press, 1909.

learning; and men in requitall honour the names of those brave Princes."[2] Of course, authors in all ages have written because of an inner urge or for self-satisfaction; but if an author sought remuneration in ancient, medieval, and Elizabethan times patronage was his source; and through these successive ages a continuous tradition is revealed which is altered only according to changes in social and economic conditions. In the age of Elizabeth, poets, printers, artists, musicians, and travelers all were dependent upon patronage, as schools, universities, and churches were maintained by it, these latter from a very different motive. To be a great gentleman like Sidney was to dispense the largess of patronage. To write a book on discovery, science, or art, to publish a song book or sequence of sonnets was to demand it. The drama, as is well known, enjoyed not only the formal patronage of noblemen of state and office, the Lord Chamberlain, the Lord High Admiral, and many others; but neither Queen Elizabeth nor her successor disdained to protect players. As to books and their dedications, Dekker remarks that it is "as common to seeke patrons to bookes, as Godfathers to children."[3] Indeed, it is conspicuous to find an Elizabethan book not dedicated to somebody, from Spenser's *Faerie Queene,* whose august patron was Elizabeth herself, to "Oblivion," to which dark and final abstraction John Marston had the impudence to dedicate his satires.

One of the earliest characteristics of the epistle dedicatory is humility. An exquisite perception of the obligations of rank pervaded everything the Elizabethan did; and in general the au-

2 Michael Drayton, "England's Heroical Epistles," 1598, *Spenser Soc.*, 1886, Vol. XLVI.

3 Thomas Dekker, "A Knight's Conjuring," 1607 (ed. Edward F. Rimbault), *Percy Soc.*, 1842, Vol. V.

thor's attitude was that expressed by George Peele in his dedication of *The Honour of the Garter,* 1593:

> Plain is my coat, and humble is my gait,
> Thrice-noble Earl; behold with gentle eyes
> My wit's poor worth.[4]

A man of talent, even genius, prostrated himself before his patron as he presented his manuscript or book.[5] The title *Churchyard's Chippes,* 1573, is indicative of this author's obsequiousness; while even the plays of the 1623 folio are referred to as "trifles"; and for venturing to print and dedicate such "toys" as plays and for daring to call them "works" Jonson was mocked by no less a competitor than Thomas Heywood.[6] In his preface to *Mamillia,* 1593, Robert Greene attacked this style of deprecatory writing, although his own work is not devoid of obsequiousness. Even the best learned of writers call their books "vanities, shadowes, imperfect patterns, more mete for the pedler than the printer, toyes, trifles, trash, trinkets, and yet the worst of them so perfectly polished with the pumice stone of eloquence."[7] In time, and especially after the publication of Sidney's *Apologie for Poetry,* 1595, authors began to assume literary dignity, and accordingly phrases of genuine modesty supplanted those conventional expressions of perfunctory humility among such writers as Barnfield, Southwell, Breton, Jonson, and Camden. A formal protest against obsequi-

4 George Peele, *The Honour of the Garter,* 1593 (ed. A. B. Dyce), 1829, II, 2. "Ad Mæcenatum Prologus."

5 See frontispiece.

6 Thomas Heywood, *The English Traveller,* 1633 (ed. John Pearsons), London. 1874, Vol. IV, "To the Reader."

7 Robert Greene, *Mamillia,* 1593 (ed. Grosart), *Huth Library,* 1881–86, Vol. II, "Dedication."

ousness was registered by Henry Porter in *The Two Angry Women of Abington*, 1599. He would ask, but he knew not how, for "to beg were base, and to cooche low and to carrie an humble shew of entreatie were too dog-like, that faunes on his master to get a bone from his trencher."[8] He could not abide it. The whole form, however, was a matter of convention inextricably bound up with patronage. Lowly submission of author to patron, the manner of servile obedience, and its none too infrequent degeneracy into sycophancy: all were a part of the conventionality of the system; and as the system broke down its accoutrements likewise fell. On the whole, literary dignity and sweet modesty describe the late Elizabethan author. But the "servility" of these old writings is largely conventional, like the subscription "your humble servant" in letters, and it is easy for us to make too much of it.

A display of affection, likewise perhaps often conventional in character, illustrates the pleasant relationship existing between author and patron. Despite the fact that verse is a more exalted medium for the expression of devotion, between the years 1590 and 1600 prose dedications of unalloyed love were somewhat fashionable. In 1590 appeared Sidney's *Arcadia* dedicated to his sister and Lodge's *Rosalynde* dedicated to Lord Hunsdon; in 1591 Fraunce's *Countess of Pembrokes Yvychurch* and *The Countess of Pembrokes Emanuell;* in 1594 Shakespeare's *Rape of Lucrece* dedicated to the Earl of Southampton; and in 1595 Bacon's *Essayes* dedicated to his brother Anthony. Sidney's and Bacon's dedications express devotion between brother and sister; but the remainder, though inscribed to literary patrons, reveal at times a charming personal relation. Probably the best representative of

8 Henry Porter, "The Two Angry Women of Abington," 1599 (ed. A. B. Dyce), *Percy Soc.*, 1861, Vol. V.

this none too conventional type is Shakespeare's *Rape of Lucrece* quoted in this anthology.

The courteous age of Sir Walter Raleigh knew how to say "thank you" most exquisitely for a favor by way of dedicatory reward. Wholesome and charming Nicholas Breton, always graceful and untiring in expressions of gratitude in his *True Description of Unthankfulnesse,* 1602, expresses a common sentiment among Elizabethan authors when he writes "Hee that is unthankful for a good turne, sheweth the venime of a vile Nature, and hee that is kindly gratefull, is worthie to bee beloved."[9] Definite cause for gratitude is not infrequently explicitly stated: Churchyard thanks the Queen for his pension; Humphrey Gifford, his master for the leisure and opportunity to produce *A Posie of Gilliflowers;* Dekker, the actors, the Queen's Majesties Servants, for their cost, counsel, and labor in producing *If It Be Not Good, The Divel Is In It;* Florio, the Ladies Lucy, Countess of Bedford, and Anne Harrington, for their hospitable house, "his retreat in storms, his relief in need";[10] Samuel Purchase, his patron, Dr. King, for the position which he procured for him; and Wither, those who visited him in the Marshalsea prison; while Holinshed, Selden, Burton, and Weever express recognition for intellectual aid in their enterprises. Selden says that he restores rather than gives Sir Robert Cotton the *History of Tithes,* 1618, because he was permitted to draw so generously on his knowledge and library. Frequently our only method of discovering a patron's generosity is through such dedications.

Despite these gentler qualities flattery was, after all, the chief

9 Nicholas Breton, *A True Description of Unthankfulnesse,* 1602.

10 John Florio, *Montaigne's Essays Englished,* 1603, *Everyman's,* 1921, Vol. I, "Dedication."

requisite of a dedication. However, literary compliments were commonly received as given, lightly and conventionally, a little more than a part of the glitter of Elizabethan life, that life ever mindful of differences of rank and the courtesy due these distinctions and not inharmonious with the silks, jewels, and farthingales of personal attire. For extravagant literary compliment, Queen Elizabeth was to no small degree responsible; few petitions succeeded unless she was hailed as a goddess. Encomiastic speeches, letters, and dedications in the supposition of dazzling beauty, eternal youth, and grace, however superfluous and inappropriate, were tendered and accepted with what to us seems equal impropriety. Compliments to Elizabeth were based not only on a recognition of her regal station, but on her intellect, her political sagacity in maintaining peace and prosperity, and for her personal charm; the first two fully warranted, but the latter even more certain to afford her the greatest personal satisfaction. Elizabeth's successor was equally open to the beguilements of the flattery of effulgent laudatory epistles. The dedication of Bacon's *Proficience and Advancement of Learning* to King James was so hyperbolic that Bacon attempted to justify it as a form due in civility to great persons, for by telling men what they are, they represent to them what they should be. Though Bacon had declared himself an enemy to flattering dedications and though he had also declared that books should have no patrons but truth and reason, his practice in this respect by no means bore out this ideal theory.

The chapter "Epistles Laudatory" of Angell Day's *English Secretorie,* 1595, prescribes the various attributes worthy of compliment: descent and family, for instance; or military prowess; intellectual attainments; virtue, personal charm, and beauty; and, in the main, dedicatory epistles emphasize these excellencies. Spenser's *Daphnaïda,* 1596, traces the genealogy of the Marquesse of Northampton; in the dedication of his translation of *Guazzo's Civil Conversation,* 1581, Pettie praises Lady Norrice's sons, whom he describes, like the Gracchi, as her jewels who "both in vertue and bewtie excelleth the richest Diamond, and the most precious Pearle that is";[11] Greene and Lodge constantly praise their patrons because they are both soldiers and scholars; Wilson, Holland, and Chapman exalt the intellectual attainments of their patrons, John Dudley, Sir Robert Cecil, and Sir Francis Bacon respectively. To be a favorer of learning was a common cause for flattery, second only to wearing the laurel crown itself. Jonson, for example, commends Prince Henry not merely for his royal birth and virtue but chiefly for his favor to letters. Greene's favorite method is to salute his patron as Mæcenas. Commendations for moral virtue are extended most profusely to the Earl of Arundel, Sir William Hatton, Lady Norrice, Lady Elizabeth Carey, the Earl of Suffolk, and William Herbert, Earl of Pembroke; while Sir Philip Sidney and his sister, Lady Mary, Countess of Pembroke, are ever the ideal of the Elizabethan heart.

The language of adulation is essentially a poetic one, and for hyperbole, metaphor, simile, and other figures of speech, authors drew on the beautiful in nature: the sun, moon, stars, the vines, flowers, trees, and birds; the rare jewels of the earth—diamonds, rubies, and pearls; the hierarchy of blessed spirits—angels and divine powers; the classic figures of mythology; and ancient kings of unusual power and brilliance. No little of the spirit of poetry is to be found in some of these prose dedications as may be dis-

11 Bartholomew Young and George Pettie, *Guazzo's Civil Conversation,* 1586 (ed. Sir Edward Sullivan), 1925, Vol. I, "Dedication," by Pettie.

covered in perusing this little volume. Among authors given more particularly to flattering dedications were Fenton, Nashe, Holland, Davies, and Chapman. Among those who felt it necessary to defend their overt bids for patronage by flattery was Churchyard who declared it was a point of wisdom, which his betters taught him, that he took an example from the fish that followed the stream.[12]

The contest among authors in the art of adroit flattery, the effort to emulate one another in hyperbolic compliment, reached its height in the decade between 1590 and 1600. At the close of the sixteenth century a reaction against all this set in, and in the second decade of the seventeenth century the revulsion against flattery became as strong as had been the earlier emulation for the rhetorical rendition of felicitous compliments. Authors who voiced their objections to flattery were Breton, Dekker, Markham, Rowlands, Wither, Rowley, Heywood, Hall, and Rich. Middleton's *Faire Quarrel,* 1617, dedicated to Robert Grey is devoid of flattery because the patron loves it not; while Heywood dedicates *The Fair Maid of the West,* printed in 1631, "without the sordid expectation of reward or servile imputation of flattery." Before the passing of the Elizabethan age the convention of hyperbolic exaggeration seems to have become almost a thing of the past, and dedications of humility and flattery were beginning to be supplanted by those more independent in tone.

Elizabethan authors may be divided into five classes: aristocratic or non-professional writers such as Greville and Sidney; men of distinct social standing holding official positions, as Spen-

12 Thomas Churchyard, "A Sparke of Friendship and Warm Good-Will," 1588, in John Nichols, *The Progresses and Public Processions of Queen Elizabeth,* London. 1823, II, 586–602.

ser, Daniel, Florio, Camden, Jonson, Beaumont, and Fletcher; men of learning and genius without recognized social position as Shakespeare, Chapman, Drayton, Lodge, Marlowe, and Webster; men of training and literary taste forced to write down as Greene, Peele, Nashe, Dekker, and Middleton; and finally hack writers such as Rowlands and Taylor.[13] But aside from this classification it is possible to trace a gradual growth in literary and financial independence among authors of the Elizabethan age. Spenser's superb dedication of his *Faerie Queene,* 1596, which is "to live with the eternity of her fame," is a perfect example of the judicious fusion of manly independence and courtesy; while the letters prefixed to Shakespeare's *Venus and Adonis,* 1593, and *The Rape of Lucrece,* 1594, are likewise not without a happy mingling of deference with self-respect. Nicholas Breton has a quiet dignity and independence of spirit, and though courteous is never subservient either to patron or reader. A growing literary dignity and independence may be traced in the dedications of Marston, Jonson, Middleton, Camden, Wither, Webster, and Heywood among others. Jonson closes the dedication of *Cynthia's Revels,* 1616, with the phrase: "Thy Servant, but not Slave"; Webster's message "To the Reader" in the *Duchess of Malfi,* 1623, declares: "I am confident this worke is not unworthy your Honors perusal for by such Poems as this, Poets have kist the hands of Great Princes, and draune their gentle eyes to looke downe upon their sheetes of paper, when the Poets themselves were bound up in their winding sheets"; while his *Devil's Law Case,* 1623, is prefaced with: "had I thought it unworthy, I had not enquired after so worthy a Patronage." Heywood's dedication of *The English Traveller,* 1633, tells his patron "Neither Sir, neede you to thinke it any under-

13 See Phoebe Sheavyn, *op. cit.,* pp. 138–139.

valuing of your worth, to undertake the patronage of a Poem in this nature"; Taylor says: "I thine, if thou mine,"[14] and Wither: "I value not thine, or any mans displeasure."[15] Camden was so independent that he could boast that he "never made suit to any man,"[16] and like Ben Jonson he refused knighthood. Authorship was assuming not only a financial but a corresponding literary dignity and independence.

To imply that without patronage there would have been no literature is an exaggeration, for authors have always written because of an inner urge or for self-satisfaction; but it is true that because of the encouragement thus given to literature we have a far richer inheritance. Authors previous to and even during Queen Elizabeth's reign could not depend on their pens alone for a livelihood, but attempted to supplement their earnings by university posts or fellowships, tutorships, teaching positions, and clerical benefices. Sometimes a publisher lodged and boarded a writer while he was engaged in correcting and editing for the press or in translating. John Foxe, author of *Acts and Monuments,* 1562, took a prominent part in the business of John Day; Nashe was provided for by John Danter, and Gabriel Harvey by John Wolfe; while Holinshed's *Chronicles of England, Scotland, and Ireland,* 1577, completed in 1586–87, and Harrison's *Description of England,* 1577, prefixed to the *Chronicles* were originally undertaken by the Queen's printer, Reginald Wolfe, who had planned "an universall cosmographie of the whole world" and employed Holinshed and Harrison to assist him.

14 John Taylor, "The Nipping or Snipping of Abuses," 1630, *Spenser Soc.,* 1869, Vol. III, "Works of John Taylor," II, 245.

15 George Wither, "Historie of the Parliament," 1650, *Spenser Soc.,* 1883, Vol. XXXVI.

16 William Camden, Letter to Ussher in 1618 (ep. 195).

Rewards bestowed on authors by patrons were of various kinds: annuities, official appointments, maintenance, hospitality, and money gifts. In the ideal state, patronage was adequate for all writers of merit; but, due to changes in social, economic, and literary conditions during the Elizabethan reign, patronage could no longer support literature as it had previously done. The growth of a middle class in prosperity demanding reading of their own, the widening popularity of poetry and especially of the drama begot writers as well as an ever increasing clientele of readers. The number of authors increased out of all proportion to the number of patrons capable of supplying adequate support. In some cases authors attempted to make up for this deficiency by means of multiple dedication; even two or three patrons were sometimes addressed. On the other hand, Barnabe Riche's *Honestie of This Age,* 1614, is dedicated to a patron unknown save through reputation. If a nobleman was reported to be generous he became subject to a storm of dedications. Though justification for choice of patron was a favorite theme in dedications, authors were not unknown to serve dedications without authorization. This resulted occasionally in an ironical choice. Gosson's *School of Abuse,* 1579, an attack on stage plays, was dedicated either in impudence or in ignorance to Sir Philip Sidney and "was for his labor scorned," Spenser tells us, "at least if it be in the goodness of that nature to scorn."[17] Gosson was promptly answered by Lodge in his *Defense of Poesy, Music, and Stage Plays;* and soon after Sidney courteously repudiated Gosson's book with his own *Apologie for Poetry* for manuscript circulation among friends. In 1599 John Hayward was imprisoned for his prose *History of Henry IV,*

17 Edmund Spenser, "Letters from Spenser (Immerito) to Gabriel Harvey, 1579–1580" (ed. Grosart), *Complete Works of Edmund Spenser,* 1882–84, IX, 263.

which he had all too effusively dedicated to the Earl of Essex; and Essex himself suffered more than once because he had been unwittingly chosen as dedicatee to tracts considered treasonable. Dekker's *Lanthorne and Candlelight,* 1608, exposes the abuses of patronage and offers a sympathetic study of the patron's problems. Complaints as registered by Churchyard, Nashe, and Barnfield; satirical, fantastical, and farcical dedications as penned by Marston, Brathwaite, Taylor, Porter, Day, and Wither assume the place of those expressive of humility, gratitude, affection, and flattery.

By the end of the sixteenth century the payment of authors had become a trade custom. The custom in Elizabethan days transferred the complete right in a manuscript to a publisher on a single outright payment, thus precluding the possibility of an author's profiting by subsequent editions unless he revised or enlarged his book. Though the ordinances of the Stationers' Company were not planned to benefit authors, they did so indirectly, for next to obtaining a copyright for himself the best thing that could befall an author was to sell to some one who could provide such, thereby making profit greater. Certain authors as Daniel, Moryson, and Wither were granted royal privileges for a period of years; the subscription method was essayed by Minsheu and Taylor; Daniel, Drayton, and Markham frequently revised their works; and Wither's *Fidelia,* 1615, definitely states one chief purpose in undertaking the work was pecuniary. Thus we see patronage could no longer carry the financial burden of authorship, and the rise of the professional man of letters had begun.

Patronage, however, had by no means ceased to exist; it was merely that the nature of its function changed. Protection rather than financial support was requested of the patron, for censorship laws were so strictly enforced that danger was discovered where none existed and a rumor was sufficient to send one to the Tower. Jonson was brought before the Lord Chief Justice for his attack on lawyers and soldiers in the play *Poetaster,* 1602, and his innocence was defended by Richard Martin to whom in kindly requital he dedicated the play in the 1616 folio edition. *The Knight of the Burning Pestle,* 1613, by Beaumont, declares "That the author had no intent to wrong any one in this comedy." The political jealousies and suspicions of the day, the religious struggles, always two-thirds political, were so vehement that slander, damaging reports, and envious tongues required the intervention of influential patrons. "Momus," a curious carper; "sycophant," he that falsely accuses an innocent; and "Zoilus," an anti-humanist, personages derived from the furniture of classical satire, to which were added the epithets "envious," "carping," "scornful," "curious," "idle," and "spiteful" were the terms authors employed in their fight with the critics from whom they begged to be saved.[18] The patron was the strong prop called upon to support the weak vine, the innocent poem or play. Under the conventionality of the phraseology lay a genuine need.

Aside from the author three functions are requisite for the production of a book; that of the capitalist who owns the manuscript and finances the enterprise, that of the craftsman who prints the book, and that of the merchant who sells it to the public. The earliest book producers exercised all three functions: publisher, printer, and bookseller; and in England he was commonly called bookseller or stationer. But before the passing of the Elizabethan era we are forced to recognize, theoretically at least, three separate persons; and the various trade arrangements are usually indi-

18 See C. H. Conley, *The First English Translators of the Classics,* Yale Univ. Press, 1927, pp. 86–94.

cated in the imprint found at the foot of the title-page. The number of printers was definitely fixed by the Stationers' Company, a government corporation. The printer was no longer a scholar who edited the books he printed, nor did he even finance them and organize their sale. These latter functions had passed to the publisher, while the printer merely performed the work for which he received pay. The general system of monopoly, favored by Queen Elizabeth, limited an author's choice of publisher for religious, legal, and educational books. Thus Richard Tottel by royal grant more or less specialized in books on common law, W. Seres in primers and psalters, Christopher and Richard Barker in Bibles, John Day under the special protection of Archbishop Parker in ecclesiastical works, William Byrd in musical publications, and John Wolfe in foreign languages. Edward Blount, friend of Marlowe; William Ponsonby, publisher of Spenser's *Faerie Queene* and of Sidney's writings; Nicholas Lynge and Cuthbert Burby were publishers of books of literary quality. Thomas Thorpe, Andrew Wise, and James Roberts accepted plays readily, while John Danter favored pamphlets and ballads. William Jaggard, printer of the pirated edition of *A Passionate Pilgrim,* 1599, none the less together with Edward Blount, the King's printer, printed the authorized Shakespearean folio of 1623.

The word "publisher," as one whose business it is to undertake the production and distribution of books, did not come into use until the eighteenth century; consequently what would now be called the "Publisher's Preface" is headed "The Stationer to the Reader." Since the stationer depended on the public for his market, he insisted on an epistle to the reader. In *The World Tost at Tennis,* 1620, Middleton tells us the printer "requested an epistle for his pass, to satisfy his perusers how hitherto he hath behaved himself." In case of the absence of such a message the stationer provided one written either by himself or by another more capable. Thus both the dedication and the epistle to the reader of the 1623 folio, indubitably penned by Ben Jonson, were signed by Heming and Condell, fellow actors of Shakespeare who were responsible for the publication of the first folio. Stationers' epistles generally praised the author and his work and aimed to establish confidential relations with prospective customers.

The signing of a dedication was an assertion of full and responsible ownership in a book. Since the modern conception of copyright had not been evolved, whoever actually possessed the manuscript was for practical purposes considered its owner; and due to manuscript circulation, made more or less promiscuous by the work of the scrivener, a publisher could readily procure a popular poem, proceed to have it registered in the Stationers' Register, print it or arrange for its printing, choose the patron, and write the dedication. Shakespeare's *Sonnets,* 1609, dedicated by Thomas Thorpe, is a case in point. In cases of posthumous publication when relatives or friends renounced or refused ownership the publisher was justified. Men who depended on their pens for a livelihood seem to have suffered very little from piracy, for the appropriation of literary rights without permission or payment was mainly concerned with posthumous publications or works of those whose rank would have forbidden acceptance of pay. And as suggested above in connection with mystification, attacks on stationers for printing without permission were frequently due to an author's reticence to subscribe his name to print and are therefore only doubtfully sincere. The Elizabethan publisher exercised unusual control over literature, for it was because of his initiative that works of genius were rescued from the perilous fragility of manuscripts to the safer shelter of printed books. He may have been destitute of present-day conceptions of rights of authors or other publishers; but instead of being censured for this, he should be commended for stimulating an interest in that great body of Elizabethan literature which he helped to preserve.

With the development of printing and the direct encouragement thus given to authorship, with the rise of the man of letters and the decline of patronage as a financial system, came a corresponding growth in importance of the stationer. Authors began to depend on publishers and they in turn depended on the general reader; therefore both alike courted their new patron the public. With increased opportunities for education for the middle and even lower classes, the reading group was no longer confined to court and gentry, but writers could safely appeal to a circle of readers of all classes. Robert Greene, for instance, appeals to an ever widening group. From 1580 to 1587 he habitually writes "To the Gentlemen Readers" or "To the Gentlemen Readers Health"; then in 1587 he writes an additional epistle for *Penelopes Web,* "To the Courteous and Courtly Ladies of England." *Greenes Mourning Garment,* 1590, appears with one "to the Gentlemen Schollers of Both Universities"; *The Royal Exchange,* 1590, "To the right honourable citizens of the Citie of London"; and *A Notable Discovery of Coosnage,* 1591, "To the Yong Gentlemen, Marchants, Apprentises, Farmers, and plain Countreymen Health." Deloney dedicates his novels "To the famous Cloth Workers in England" or "To the Master and Wardens of the worshipfull company of Cordwaynors," and writes as an artisan for the jolly companions of his craft with whom he had worked at his loom in Norwich. In 1613 Thomas Campion addresses his *Songs of Mourning* "To the World" and in 1622 Drayton his

Poly-olbion "To any that will read it." The 1623 folio is addressed to readers "from the most able to him that can but spell."

The attitude to the reader marks a development in prefatory writing. Churchyard, one of the early Elizabethans, is condescending in tone. Apprehension shows in Breton who emphasizes the difficulty of pleasing so many tastes. Indifference, real or feigned, appears in the work of Gifford, Marston, Giles Fletcher (the elder), and Barnabe Riche. Lodge, Dekker, and Drayton do not hesitate to rebuke the reader; while Scoloker, Day, and Webster become satirical. But epistles signed by the stationer reveal him as a man of business whose duty it is to establish friendly relationships in order to encourage buyers. The complete emancipation of the professional writer was secured by the continued growth of the book-buying public till publishers could secure sufficient profit to pay authors an adequate income for their support. A. W. Pollard says it took three centuries wholly to supersede patronage, and in Shakespeare's day only about a third of the road had been traveled.[19]

19 See Alfred W. Pollard, *Shakespeare's Fight with the Pirates and the Problems of the Transmission of His Text,* London. 1917. Ch. II, "Authors, Players, and Pirates in Shakespeare's Day."

DEDICATIONS AND PREFACES

Tottel's Miscellany, 1557.

The Printer to the Reader.

THAT to have wel written in verse, yea & in small parcelles, deserveth great praise, the workes of divers Latines, Italians, and other, doe prove sufficiently. That our tong is able in that kynde to do as praiseworthely as ye rest, the honorable stile of the noble earle of Surrey, and the weightinesse of the depewitted sir Thomas Wyat the elders verse, with severall graces in sondry good Englishe writers, doe show abundantly. It resteth nowe (gentle reder) that thou thinke it not evill doon, to publish, to the honor of the Englishe tong, and for profit of the studious of Englishe eloquence, those workes which the ungentle horders up of such treasure have heretofore envied thee. And for this point (good reder) thine own profit and pleasure, in these presently, and in moe hereafter, shal answere for my defence. If parhappes some mislike the statelinesse of stile removed from the rude skill of common eares, I aske help of the learned to defend their learned frendes, the authors of this work. And I exhort the unlearned, by reding to learne to be more skilfull, and to purge that swinelike grossenesse, that maketh the sweet ma[j]ierome not to smell to their delight.

John Stow, *Summary of English Chronicles,* 1565.

To the Reader.

DIVERS wryters of Hystories write dyversly. Some penne their hystories plentifully at large. Some contrary wyse, briefly and shortly doo but (as it were) touche by the way, the remembraunce and accidents of those tymes of which they write. Some do with a large compasse discover as wel the affaires done in foreyn partes, as those that hapned in that countrey of whiche especially they wryte. And some, content to let alone other matters, put in memory only such thyngs, as they them selves have had experience of in their own countreis. Amongs whom, good Reader, I crave to have place, and desyre roome in the lower part of this table. For I use thee in this my booke as some symple feaster, that beynge not able of his owne coste to feast his guestes sufficientely, is fayne to bee frended of his neyghboures, and to sette before them suche dishes as he hath gotten of others. For I acknowledge, that many of the hystories that thou shalte reade here abridged are taken partely out of Robert Fabian, sometyme Alderman of London, Edwarde Halle gentylman of Greyes Inne, John Hardynge, a great travailer bothe in foreyne countreis, and also in all writynges of antiquitie: and other, who reaped great abundance of knowledge, and filled their bookes full therwith, to the great profite and pleasure of all posteritie, and to their own great fame and glory. So that of their great plenty, I might wel take somewhat to hyde my povertie. Howbe it, I have not so doone it, as, if they should clayme theyr own, I shuld forthwith be left naked. For somwhat I have noted, which I my selfe, partly by paynfull searche, and partly by diligent experience, have found out. Wherfore, both the smalnesse of the volume, which comprehendeth gret matters in effect, also the noveltie of som matters uttred therin, ought to cause it, it shold not be altogither unwelcome to thee. For, though it be written homely, yet it is not (as I trust) writen untruly. And in hystories the chiefe thyng that is to be desyred is truthe. Wherfore, if thou fynde that in it, I beseche thee, wynke at small faultes, or at the least, let the consyderation of my well meanynge drowne them. So shalt thou both encourage me to farther diligence, and also utter thyne owne frendlynesse, in that thou doest rather further, then condemne a weake wryter.

Of smoothe and flatterynge speache, remember to take hede:
For Trouthe in playn wordes may be tolde, of craft a lye hath nede.

Roger Ascham, *The Scholemaster*, 1570.

To the honorable Sir William Cecill Knight, principall Secretarie to the Quenes most excellent Majestie.

SONDRY *& reasonable be the causes why learned men have used to offer and dedicate such workes as they put abrode to some such personage as they thinke fittest, either in respect of abilitie of defense, or skill for jugement, or private regard of kindenesse and dutie. Every one of those considerations, Syr, move me of right to offer this my late husbands* M. Aschams *worke unto you. For well remembryng how much all good learnyng oweth unto you for defense therof, as the Universitie of Cambrige, of which my said late husband was a member, have in chosing you their worthy Chaunceller acknowledged, and how happily you have spent your time in such studies & caried the use therof to the right ende, to the good service of the Quenes Majestie and your contrey to all our benefites, thyrdly how much my sayd husband was many wayes bound unto you, and how gladly and comfortably he used in hys lyfe to recognise and report your goodnesse toward hym, leavyng with me then hys poore widow and a great sort of orphanes a good comfort in the hope of your good continuance, which I have truly found to me and myne, and therfore do duely and dayly pray for you and yours:*

I could not finde any man for whose name this booke was more agreable for hope [of] protection, more mete for submission to judgement, nor more due for respect of worthynesse of your part and thankefulnesse of my husbandes and myne. Good I trust it shall do, as I am put in great hope by many very well learned that can well judge therof. Mete therefore I compt it that such good as my husband was able to do and leave to the common weale, it should be received under your name, and that the world should owe thanke therof to you to whom my husband the authour of it was for good receyved of you, most dutiefully bounden. And so besechyng you, to take on you the defense of this booke, to avaunce the good that may come of it by your allowance and furtherance to publike use and benefite, and to accept the thankefull recognition of me and my poore children, trustyng of the continuance of your good memorie of M. Ascham *and his, and dayly commendyng the prosperous estate of you and yours to God whom you serve and whoes you are, I rest to trouble you.*

Your humble Margaret
Ascham.

Thomas Norton and Thomas Sackville, *Gorboduc*, 1570.

The P. to the Reader.

WHERE this Tragedie was for furniture of part of the grand Christmasse in the Inner Temple first written about nine yeares agoe by the right honourable Thomas now Lorde Buckherst, and by T. Norton, and after shewed before her Majestie, and never intended by the authors therof to be published: yet one W. G. getting a copie therof at some yongmans hand that lacked a litle money and much discretion, in the last great plage, an. 1565. about V. yeares past, while the said Lord was out of England, and T. Norton farre out of London, and neither of them both made privie, put it forth excedingly corrupted: even as if by meanes of a broker for hire, he should have entised into his house a faire maide and done her villanie, and after all to bescratched her face, torne her apparell, berayed and disfigured her, and then thrust her out of dores dishonested. In such plight after long wandring she came at length home to the sight of her frendes who scant knew her but by a few tokens and markes remayning. They, the authors, I meane, though they were very much displeased that she so ranne abroad without leave, whereby she caught her shame, as many wantons do, yet seing the case as it is remedilesse, have for common honestie and shamefastnesse new apparelled, trimmed, and attired her in such forme as she was before, in which better forme since she hath come to me. I have harbored her for her frendes' sake and her owne, and I do not dout her parentes, the authors, will not now be discontent that she goe abroad among you good readers so it be in honest companie. For she is by my encouragement and others somewhat lesse ashamed of the dishonestie done to her because it was by fraude and force. If she be welcome among you and gently enterteined in favor of the house from whense she is descended, and of her owne nature courteously disposed to offend no man, her frendes will thanke you for it. If not, but that she shall be still reproched with her former missehap, or quarelled at by envious persons, the poore gentlewoma[n] wil surely play Lucreces part & of her self die for shame, and I shall wishe that she had taried still at home with me, where she was welcome: for she did never put me to more charge, but this one poore blacke gowne lined with white that I have now geven her to goe abroad among you withall.

George Gascoigne, *A Hundreth Sundrie Flowers,* 1572.

The Printer to the Reader.

IT hath bin an old saying, that whiles two doggs do strive for a bone, the thirde may come and carie it away. And this proverbe may (as I feare) be wel verefied in me which take in hand the imprinting of this poeticall Poesie. For the case seemeth doubtful, and I will disclose my conjecture. Master. H. W. in the beginning of this worke, hath in his letter (written to the Readers) cunningly discharged himselfe of any such misliking as the graver sort of grey-heared judgers mighte (perhaps) conceive in the publication of these pleasant Pamphlets. And nexte unto that learned preamble, the letter of. G. T. (by whome as seemeth, the first coppie hereof was unto the same. H. W. delivered) doth with no lesse clerkly cunning seeke to perswade the readers that he (also) woulde by no meanes have it published. Now I feare very muche (all these words notwithstanding) that these two gentlemen were of one assent compact to have it imprinted; and yet, finding by experience that nothing is so wel handled now adayes, but that some malicious minds may either take occasion to mislike it themselves, or else finde meanes to make it odious unto others, they have therefore (each of them) politiquely prevented the daunger of misreport and suffered me the poore Printer to runne away with the palme of so perillous a victorie. Notwithstanding, having wel perused the worke, I find nothing therein amisse (to my judgemente) unlesse it be two or three wanton places passed over in the discourse of an amorous enterprise, the which for as much as the words are cleanly (although the thing ment be somewhat naturall) I have thought good also to let them passe as they came to me, and the rather bicause (as master. H. W. hath well alleadged in his letter to the Reader) the well minded man may reape some commoditie out of the most frivolous works that are written. And as the venemous spider will sucke poison out of the most holesome herbe, and the industrious Bee can gather hony out of the most stinking weede, even so the discrete reader may take a happie example by the most lascivious histories, although the captious and harebraind heads can neither be encoraged by the good, nor forewarned by the bad. And thus muche I have thought good to say in excuse of some savours, which may perchance smell unpleasantly to some noses, in some part of this poeticall poesie. Now it hath with this fault a greater commoditie than common poesies have ben accustomed to present, and that is this, you shall not be constreined to smell of the floures therein conteined all at once, neither yet to take them up in such order as they are sorted; but you may take any one flowre by itselfe, and if that smell not so pleasantly as you wold wish, I doubt not yet but you may find some other which may supplie the defects thereof. As thus, he which wold have good morall lessons clerkly handled, let him smell to the Tragedie translated out of Euripides. He that wold laugh at a prety conceit closely conveyed, let him peruse the comedie translated out of Ariosto. He that would take example by the unlawfull affections of a lover bestowed uppon an unconstant dame, let them reade the report in verse, made by Dan Bartholmew of Bathe, or the discourse in prose of the adventures passed by master F. I. whome the reader may name Freeman Jones, for the better understanding of the same. He that would see any particuler pang of love lively displayed, may here approve every Pamphlet by the title, and so remaine contented; as also divers godly himnes and Psalmes may in like manner be founde in this recorde. To conclude, the worke is so universall, as either in one place or other, any mans mind may therewith be satisfied. The which I adventure (under pretext of this promise) to present unto all indifferent eyes as followeth.

(·.·)

The Paradyse of Daynty Devises, 1576.

TO THE RIGHT HONO-rable Syr Henry Compton Knight,

Lorde Compton, of Compton.

RIGHT HONORABLE, *and my very good Lord, (presuming uppon your curtesy) I am bolde to present unto your honor, this small volume: Entituled, The Paradise of deynty devises, being penned by divers learned Gentlemen, and collected togeather, through the travell of one, both of woorship and credite, for his private use: who not long since departed this lyfe, which when I had perused over, not with out the advise of sundry my freendes, I determined by theyr good motion, to set them in print, who therunto greatly perswaded me, with these and like woordes: The wryters of them were both of honor and worship: besides that, our owne countrey men, and such as for theyr learnyng and gravitie might be accounted of among the wisest. Furthermore, the ditties both pithy and pleasant, aswell for the invention as meter, and wyll yeelde a farre greater delight, being as they are so aptly made to be set to any song in .5. partes, or song to instrument. Which wel consydering, I purposed not to forsake so good an occasion, beseeching your honor to accept it in good part, cheefely for the aucthours sake: who though some of them are departed this lyfe, yet theyr woorthy doings shall con-*

tinue for ever: for like as the shadow foloweth the body, so praise foloweth vertue: and as the shadow goeth somtimes before, and sometimes behind, so doth praise also to vertue: but the later it commeth, the greater it is, and to be the better esteemed. Thus fearing to offende your honor with these my rude speaches, I end, wishing your L. many yeres of joy.

Your good Lordships wholy to commaund.

H. D.

Robert Cary, *Memoirs*, 1577–1625.

O LORD my God, open mine eyes, and enlarge my heart, with a true understanding of thy great mercyes, that thou hast blessed mee withall, from my first being untill this my old age: and give mee of thy grace to call to minde in some measure thy great and manifold blessings, that thou hast blessed mee withall; though my weaknesse be such, and my memory so short, as I have no abilities to expresse them as I ought to do, yet Lord bee pleased to accept of this sacrifice of praise and thankesgiving.

George Whetstone, *Promos and Cassandra,* 1578.

TO HIS WORSHIPFULL friende and Kinseman, *William Fleetewoode Esquier, Recorder* of London.

SYR, (desirous to acquite your tryed frendships with some token of good will) of late I perused divers of my unperfect workes, fully minded to bestowe on you the travell of some of my forepassed time. But (resolved to accompanye the adventurous Captaine Syr *Humfrey Gylbert* in his honorable voiadge) I found my leysure too littel to correct the errors in my sayd workes. So that (inforced) I lefte them disparsed amonge my learned freendes, at theyr leasure to polish, if I faild to returne: spoyling (by this meanes) my studdy of his necessarye furnyture. Amonge other unregarded papers, I fownde this Discource of *Promos* and *Cassandra;* which for the rarenesse (& the needeful knowledge) of the necessary matter contained therein (to make the actions appeare more lively) I devided the whole history into two Commedies, for that, *Decorum* used, it would not be convayed in one. The effects of both are good and bad: vertue intermyxt with vice, unlawfull desyres (if it were possible) queancht with chaste denyals: al needeful actions (I thinke) for publike vewe. For by the rewarde of the good, the good are encouraged in wel doinge: and with the scowrge of the lewde, the lewde are feared from evill attempts: mainetayning this my oppinion with *Platoes* auctority. *Nawghtinesse commes of the corruption of nature, and not by readinge or hearinge the lives of the good or lewde (for such publication is necessarye), but goodnesse (sayth he) is beawtifyed by either action.* And to these endes *Menander, Plautus,* and *Terence,* them selves many yeares since intombed, (by their Commedies) in honour live at this daye. The auncient *Romanes* heald these showes of suche prise that they not onely allowde the publike exercise of them, but the grave Senators themselves countenaunced the Actors with their presence: who from these trifles wonne morallytye, as the Bee suckes honny from weedes. But the advised devises of auncient Poets, disc[r]edited with tryfels of yonge, unadvised, and rashe witted wryters, hath brought this commendable exercise in mislike. For at this daye, the *Italian* is so lascivious in his commedies that honest hearers are greeved at his actions: the *Frenchman* and *Spaniarde* folowes the *Italians* humor: the *Germaine* is too holye, for he presentes on everye common Stage what Preachers should pronounce in Pulpets. The *Englishman* in this quallitie is most vaine, indiscreete, and out of order: he fyrst groundes his worke on impossibilities; then in three howers ronnes he throwe the worlde, marryes, gets Children, makes Children men, men to conquer kingdomes, murder Monsters, and bringeth Gods from Heaven, and fetcheth Divels from Hel. And (that which is worst) their ground is not so unperfect as their workinge indiscreete: not waying, so the people laugh, though they laugh them (for theyr follyes) to scorne. Manye tymes (to make mirthe) they make a Clowne companion with a Kinge; in theyr grave Counsels they allow the advise of fooles; yea, they use one order of speach for all persons: a grose

Indecorum, for a Crowe wyll ill counterfet the Nightingales sweete voice; even so affected speeche doth misbecome a Clowne. For, to worke a Commedie kindly, grave olde men should instruct, yonge men should showe the imperfections of youth, Strumpets should be lascivious, Boyes unhappy, and Clownes should speake disorderlye: entermingling all these actions in such sorte as the grave matter may instruct and the pleasant delight; for without this chaunge the attention would be small, and the likinge lesse.

But leave I this rehearsall of the use and abuse of Commedies, least that I checke that in others which I cannot amend in my selfe. But this I am assured, what actions so ever passeth in this History, either merry or morneful, grave or lascivious, the conclusion showes the confusion of Vice and the cherishing of Vertue. And sythe the end tends to this good, although the worke (because of evel handlinge) be unworthy your learned Censure, allowe (I beseeche you) of my good wyll, untyl leasure serves me to perfect some labour of more worthe. No more, but that almightye God be your protector, and preserve me from dainger in this voiadge, the xxix of July, 1578.

Your Kinsman to use,

George Whetstone

Stephen Gosson, *The School of Abuse*, 1579.

To the right noble Gentleman, Master Philip Sidney *Esquier, Stephan Gosson wisheth health* of body, wealth of minde, rewarde of vertue, advauncement of honour, and good successe in godly affaires.

CALIGULA, lying in Fraunce with a greate armie of fighting menne, brought all his force, on a sudden to the Sea side, as though hee intended to cutte over, and invade Englande. When he came to the shore, his Souldiers were presently set in araye, him selfe, shipped in a small barke, weyed Ancors, and lanched out. He had not played long in the Sea, wafting too and fro, at his pleasure, but he returned agayne, stroke sayle, gave allarme to his souldiers in token of battaile, & charged everie man too gather cockles. I knowe not (right worshipfull) whether my selfe be as frantike as Caligula in my proceedings, because that after I have set out the flag of defiance to some abuses, I may seeme well ynough too strike up the drumme, and bring all my power to a vaine skirmishe. The title of my book doth promise much, the volume, you see, is very little; & sithens I can not beare out my follie by authoritie, like an Emperour, I wil crave pardon for my Phrenzie, by submission, as your woorshippes too commaunde. The Schoole which I builde, is narrowe, and at the firste blushe appeareth but a doggehole; yet small Cloudes carie water; slender threedes sowe sure stitches; little heares have their shadowes; blunt stones whette knives; from hard rockes flowe soft springes; the whole worlde is drawen in a mappe; Homers Iliades in a nutte shell; a Kings picture in a pennie. Little Chestes may holde greate Treasure; a fewe Cyphers contayne the substance of a rich Merchant. The shortest Pamphlette maye shrowde matter. The hardest heade may give light, and the harshest penne maye sette downe somewhat woorth the reading.

Hee that hath bin shooke with a fierce ague, giveth good counsell to his friends when he is wel. When Ovid had roaved long on the Seas of wantonnesse, hee became a good Pilot to all that followed, and printed a carde of everie daunger; and I perswade my selfe, that seeing the abuses which I reveale, trying them thorowly to my hurt, and bearing the stench of them yet in my owne nose, I may best make the frame, found the schoole, and reade the first lecture of all my selfe, too warne every man to avoyde the perill. Wherein I am contrary to Simonides, for hee was ever slowe to utter, and swift to conceale, beeing more sorrowefull that he had spoken, then that hee had held his peace. But I accuse my selfe of discourtesie too my friendes, in keeping these abuses so long secret, and nowe thinke my duetie discharged in layinge them open.

A good Physition, when the disease cannot bee cured within, thrusteth the corruption out in the face, and delivereth his Patient to the Chirurgion. Though my skill in Physicke bee small, I have some experience in these maladyes, which I thrust out with my penne too every mans viewe, yeelding the ranke fleshe to the

Chirurgions knife, and so ridde my handes of the cure, for it passeth my cunning too heale them privily.

If your Worshippe vouchsafe to enter the Schoole doore, and walke an hower or twaine within for your pleasure, you shall see what I teach, which presente my Schoole, my cunning, and my selfe to your worthy Patronage; beseeching you, though I bidde you to Dinner, not to looke for a feast fit for the curious taste of a perfect Courtier, but too imitate Philip of Macedon, who, beeing invited to a Farmers house, when hee came from Hunting, brought a greater trayne than the poore man looked for. When they were sette, the good Philip, perceiving his Hoste sorowfull for want of meate to satisfie so many, exhorted his friends to keepe their stomackes for the seconde course; whereuppon every man fedde modestly on that whiche stoode before him, and lefte meate inough at the taking uppe of the table. And I trust if your Worshippe feede sparingly on this (too comforte your poore Hoste) in hope of a better course heereafter, though the Dishes be fewe that I set before you, they shall for this time suffice your selfe & a great many moe.

Your Worshippes to
commaund, *Stephan*
Gosson.

Stephen Gosson, *The School of Abuse,* 1579.

To the Reader.

GENTLEMEN and others, you may wel thinke that I sell you my corne and eate Chaffe, batrer my wine & drinke Water, sith I take upon mee to drive you from Playes, when mine owne woorkes are dayly to be seene upon stages as sufficient witnesses of mine owne folly and severe Judges againste my selfe. But if you sawe how many teares of sorrowe mine eyes shed when I beholde them, or how many drops of blood my heart sweates when I remember them, you would not so much blame me for missespending my time when I knew not what I did, as commend mee at the laste for recovering my steppes with graver counsell. After-wittes are ever best: burnt Children dread the fire. I have seene that which you behold, & I shun that which you frequent. And that I might the easier pull your mindes from such studyes, drawe your feete from such places, I have sente you a Schoole of those abuses which I have gathered by observation.

Theodorus, the Atheist, complayned that his schollers were woont, how plaine soever he spake, to misconster him, howe right soever hee wrote, to wrest him. And I looke for some such Auditors in my Schoole, as of rancour will hit me, how soever I warde, or of stomake assayle mee, howe soever I bee garded; making black of white, Chalke of Cheese, the full Moone of a messe of Cruddes. These are such as, with curst Curres, barke at every man but their owne friendes; these snatch up bones in open streetes, and byte them with madnesse in secrete corners: these, with sharpe windes, pearce subtiler in narrowe lanes then in large fieldes. And sith there is neither authoritie in me to bridle their tongues, nor reason in them to rule their owne talke, I am contented to suffer their taunts, requesting you, which are Gentlemen, of curtesie to beare with me, and because you are learned amende the faultes freendly which escape the Presse. The ignoraunt I knowe will swallow them downe and digest them with ease. Farewel.

Yours Stephan
Gosson.

John Lyly, *Euphues, The Anatomy of Wit*, 1579.

To the Gentlemen Readers

I WAS driven into a quandarie, Gentlemen, whether I might send this my Pamphlet to the Printer or to the pedler. I thought it to bad for the presse, & to good for the packe. But seing my folly in writing to be as great as others, I was willing my fortune should be as ill as any mans. We commonly see the booke that at Christmas lyeth bound on the Stacioners stall, at Easter to be broken in the Haberdasshers shop, which sith it is the order of proceding, I am content this winter to have my doings read for a toye, that in sommer they may be ready for trash. It is not straunge when as the greatest wonder lasteth but nyne dayes, that a newe worke should not endure but three monethes. Gentlemen use bookes, as gentlewomen handle theyr flowres, who in the morning sticke them in their heads, and at night strawe them at their heeles. Cheries be fulsome when they be through rype, bicause they be plenty, & bookes be stale when they be printed, in that they be common. In my mynde Printers and Taylors are bound chiefely to pray for Gentlemen, the one hath so many fantasies to print, the other such divers fashions to make, that the pressing yron of the one is never out of the fyre, nor the printing presse of the other any tyme lyeth still. But a fashion is but a dayes wearing, and a booke but an howres reading, which seeing it is so, I am of a shomakers mynde, who careth not so the shooe hold the plucking on, and I, so my labours last the running over. He that commeth in print bicause he would be knowen, is lyke the foole that commeth into the market bicause he would be seene. I am not he that seeketh prayse for his labour, but pardon for his offence, neither doe I set this foorth for any devotion in print, but for dutie which I owe to my Patrone. If one write never so well, he cannot please all, and write he never so ill hee shall please some. Fine heads will pick a quarrell with me if all be not curious, and flatterers a thanke, if any thing be currant. But this is my mynde, let him that fyndeth fault amende it, and him that liketh it, use it. Envie braggeth but draweth no bloud, the malicious have more mynde to quippe, then might to cut. I submit my selfe to the judgement of the wise, and I little esteme the censure of fooles. The one will be satisfyed with reason, the other are to be aunswered with silence. I know gentlemen wil fynde no fault without cause, and beare with those that deserve blame, as for others, I care not for their jestes, for I never ment to make them my Judges.

Farewell.

Sir Thomas North, *The Lives of the Noble Grecians and Romanes,* 1579.

TO THE MOST HIGH AND MIGHTY PRINCESSE ELIZABETH, BY THE GRACE OF GOD, OF ENGLAND,

Fraunce, and Ireland Queene, defender of the faith: &c.

UNDER hope of your highnes gratious and accustomed favor, I have presumed to present here unto your Majestie, Plutarkes lyves translated, as a booke fit to be protected by your highnes, and meete to be set forth in Englishe. For who is fitter to give countenance to so many great states than such an highe and mightie Princesse? Who is fitter to revive the dead memorie of their fame than she that beareth the lively image of their vertues? Who is fitter to authorize a worke of so great learning and wisedome than she whome all do honor as the Muse of the world? Therefore I humbly beseech your Majestie, to suffer the simplenes of my translation to be covered under the amplenes of your highnes protection. For, most gracious Sovereigne, though this booke be no booke for your Majesties selfe, who are meeter to be the chiefe storie, than a student therein, and can better understand it in Greeke, than any man can make it Englishe: yet I hope the common sorte of your subjects, shall not onely profit them selves hereby, but also be animated to the better service of your Majestie. For amonge all the profane bookes that are in reputacion at this day, there is none (your highnes best knowes) that teacheth so much honor, love, obedience, reverence, zeale, and devocion to Princes, as these lives of Plutarke doe. Howe many examples shall your subjects reade here, of severall persons, and whole armyes, of noble and base, of younge and olde, that both by sea & lande, at home and abroad, have strayned their wits, not regarded their states, ventured their persons, cast away their lives, not onely for the honor and safetie, but also for the pleasure of their Princes?

Then well may the Readers thinke, if they have done this for heathen Kings, what should we doe for Christian Princes? If they have done this for glorye, what shoulde we doe for religion? If they have done this without hope of heaven, what should we doe that looke for immortalitie? And so adding the encouragement of these exsamples, to the forwardnes of their owne dispositions: what service is there in warre, what honor in peace, which they will not be ready to doe for their worthy Queene?

And therefore that your highnes may give grace to the booke, and the booke may doe his service to your Majestie: I have translated it out of French, and doe here most humbly present the same unto your highnes, beseeching your Majestie with all humilitie, not to reject the good meaning, but to pardon the errours of your most humble and obedient subject and servaunt, who prayeth God long to multiplye all graces and blessings upon your Majestie. Written the sixteene day of January. 1579.

Your Majesties most humble and obedient servaunt,

Thomas North.

Richard Mulcaster, *Positions,* 1581.

TO THE MOST VERTU-OUS LADIE, HIS MOST DEARE, AND soveraine princesse, Elizabeth by the grace of God Queene of England, Fraunce, and Ireland, defendresse of the faith &c.

MY booke by the argument, most excellent princesse, pretendeth a common good, bycause it concerneth the generall traine and bringing up of youth, both to enrich their minds with learning, and to enable their bodies with health; and it craves the favour of some speciall countenaunce farre above the common, or else it can not possiblie procure free passage. For what a simple credit is myne to perswade so great a matter? Or what force is there in common patronage to commaunde conceites? I am therefore driven upon these so violent considerations to presume so farre as to present it, being my first travell that ever durst venture upon the print, unto your majesties most sacred handes. For in neede of countenaunce, where best abilitie is most assurance, and knowne vertue the fairest warrant, who is more sufficient then your excellencie is, either for cunning to commend, or for credit to commaunde? And what reason is there more likely to procure the favour of your majesties most gracious countenance, either to commende the worke, or to commaunde it waie, then the honest pretence of a generall good wherein you cannot be deceived? For of your accustomed care you will circumspectlie consider, and by your singular judgement, you can skillfully discerne, whether there be any appearance, that my booke shall performe so great a good, as it pretendeth to do before you either praise it or procure it passage. In deede it is an argument which craveth consideration, bycause it is the leader to a further consequence; and all your majesties time is so busily employed, about many and maine affaires of your estate, as I may seeme verie injurious to the common weale, besides some wrong offered to your owne person, to desire your Majestie at this time to reade any part therof, much lesse the whole, the booke it selfe being very long, & your Majesties leasure being very litle. And yet if it maye please your most excellent Majestie of some extraordinarie grace towardes a most obsequious subject in way of encoraging his both toilsome and troublesome labour, to take but some taste of any one title, of smallest encumbraunce, by the very inscription, the paw of a Lion may bewraie the hole body in me by the proverbe, in your highnesse by the propertie, as who can best judge, what the Lion is. For the rest, which neither your Majesties time can tarie on, neither my boldnesse dare desire that you should: other mens report, which shall have time to read and will lend an officious countrieman some parte of their leysure, will prove a referendarie, and certifie your highnesse how they finde me appointed. I have entitled the booke POSITIONS, bycause entending to go on further, for the avauncement of learning I thought it good at the first to put downe certaine groundes very needefull for my purpose, for that they be the common circunstances, that belong to teaching and are to be resolved on, eare we begin to teach. Wherin I crave consent of my countrey, to joyne with me in conceit, if my reasons prove likely, that therby I may direct my whole currant in the rest a great deale the better. Now if it maye stand with your Majesties most gracious good will to bestow upon me the favourable smile of your good liking, to countenance me in this course, which as it pretendeth the publike commoditie, so it threatneth me with extreme paines, all my paine will prove pleasant unto me, and that good which shall come thereby to the common weale shall be most justly ascribed to your Majesties especial goodnesse, which encoraged my labour and commended it to my countrey. Which both encoragement to my selfe, and commendacion to my countrey, I do nothing doubt but to obtaine at your Majesties most gracious handes, whether of your good nature, which hath alwaye furthered honest attemptes: or of your Princely conceit, which is thoroughly bent to the bettering of your state, considering my travell doth tend that way. For the very ende of my whole labour (if my small power can attaine to that, which a great good will towards this my cuntrey hath deepely conceived) is to helpe to bring the generall teaching in your Majesties dominions, to some one good and profitable uniformitie which now in the middest of great varietie doth either hinder much, or profit litle, or at the least nothing so much, as it were like to do, if it were reduced to one certaine fourme. The effecting wherof pretendeth great honour to your Majesties person, besides the profit, which your whole realme is to reape therby. That noble Prince king HENRY the eight, your Majesties most renowned father vouchesafed to bring all Grammers into one fourme, the multitude therof being some impediment to schoole learning in his happie time, and thereby both purchased himselfe great honour, and procured his subjectes a marveilous ease. Now if it shall please your Majestie by that Royall example which otherwise you so rarely exceede, to further not onely the helping of that booke to a refining, but also the reducing of all other schoole bookes to some better choice, and all manner of teaching, to some redier fourme, can so great a good but sound to your Majesties most endlesse renowne, whose least part gave such cause of honour, to that famous King, your Majesties father? By these few wordes your highnesse conceiveth my full meaning I am well assured, neither do I doubt, but that as you are well able to discerne it, so you will very depelie consider it, & see this so great a common good thoroughly set on foote. I know your Majesties pacience to be exceeding great in verie petie arguments, if not, I should have bene afraid to have troubled you with so many wordes, and yet least tediousnesse do soure even a sweete and sound matter, I will be no bolder. God blesse your Majestie, and send you a long, & an healthfull life, to his greatest glorie, and your Majesties most lasting honour.

Your Majesties most humble and
obedient subject
Richard Mulcaster.

King James, *Ane Schort Treatise,* 1584.

THE PREFACE TO *the Reader.*

THE cause why (docile Reader) I have not dedicat this short treatise to any particular personis (as commounly workis usis to be) is, that I esteme all thais quha hes already some beginning of knawledge, with ane earnest desyre to atteyne to farther, alyke meit for the reading of this worke, or any uther, quhilk may help thame to the atteining to thair foirsaid desyre. Bot as to this work, quhilk is intitulit *The Reulis and cautelis to be observit and eschewit in Scottis Poesie,* ye may marvell paraventure, quhairfore I sould have writtin in that mater, sen so mony learnit men, baith of auld and of late, hes already written thairof in dyvers and sindry languages: I answer that, nochtwithstanding, I have lykewayis writtin of it, for twa caussis. The ane is: As for them that wrait of auld, lyke as the tyme is changeit sensyne, sa is the ordour of Poesie changeit. For then they observit not *Flowing,* nor eschewit not *Ryming in termes,* besydes sindrie uther thingis, quhilk now we observe and eschew, and dois weil in sa doing: because that now, quhen the warld is waxit auld, we have all their opinionis in writ, quhilk were learned before our tyme, besydes our awin ingynis, quhair as they then did it onelie be thair awin ingynis, but help of any uther. Thairfore, quhat I speik of Poesie now, I speik of it as being come to mannis age and perfectioun, quhair as then it was bot in the infancie and chyldheid. The uther cause is: That as for thame that hes written in it of late, there hes never ane of thame written in our language. For albeit sindrie hes written of it in English, quhilk is lykest to our language, yet we differ from thame in sindrie reulis of Poesie, as ye will find be experience. I have lykewayis omittit dyvers figures, quhilkis are necessare to be usit in verse, for twa causis. The ane is, because they are usit in all languages, and thairfore are spokin of be *Du Bellay,* and sindrie utheris, quha hes written in this airt. Quhairfore, gif I wrait of them also, it sould seme that I did bot repete that quhilk thay have written, and yit not sa weil as they have done already. The uther cause is that they are figures of Rhetorique and Dialectique, quhilkis airtis I professe nocht, and thairfore will apply to my selfe the counsale quhilk *Apelles* gave to the shoomaker, quhen he said to him, seing him find falt with the shankis of the Image of *Venus,* efter that he had found falt with the pantoun, *Ne sutor ultra crepidam.*

I will also wish yow (docile Reidar) that, or ye cummer yow with reiding thir reulis, ye may find in your self sic a beginning of Nature as ye may put in practise in your verse many of thir foirsaidis preceptis, or ever ye sie them as they are heir set doun. For gif Nature be nocht the cheif worker in this airt, Reulis wilbe bot a band to Nature, and wil mak yow within short space weary of the haill airt: quhair as, gif Nature be cheif, and bent to it, reulis will be ane help and staff to Nature. I will end heir, lest my preface be langer nor my purpose and haill mater following: wishing yow, docile Reidar, als gude succes and great proffeit by reiding this short treatise as I tuke earnist and willing panis to blok it, as ye sie, for your cause. Fare weill.

I HAVE insert in the hinder end of this Treatise maist kyndis of versis quhilks are not cuttit or brokin, bot alyke many feit in everie lyne of the verse, and how they are commounly namit, with my opinioun for quhat subjectis ilk kynde of thir verse is meitest to be usit.

To knaw the quantitie of your lang or short fete in they lynes, quhilk I have put in the reule quhilk teachis yow to knaw quhat is *Flowing,* I have markit the lang fute with this mark —, and abone the heid of the shorte fute, I have put this mark ∪.

* *
*

William Warner, *Albions England,* 1586–1612.

To the right Honorable, my very good Lord and Maister, *Henrie Carey, Baron of Hunsdon: Knight* of the most noble Order of the Garter: Lord Chamberlaine *of her Majesties most Honorable Houshold: Lord* Governour of *Barwicke:* Lord Warden of the East Marches for *and anempst* Scotland: *Lord Lieftennant of* Suffolke *and Norfolke:* Captaine of her Majesties Gentlemen Pencioners: and one of her Highnes most Honorable Privie Councell.

THIS our whole Iland, *anciently called* Brutaine, *but more anciently* Albion, *presently containing two Kingdomes,* England *and* Scotland, *is cause (right Honorable) that to distinguish the former, whose only Occurrents I abridge, from the other, remote from our Historie, I intitle this my Booke* Albions England; *a Subject, in troth (if self conceit work not me a partial Judge) worthie your Honorable Patronage, howbeit basely passed under so badd an Author. But for great Personages gratefully to intertain the good willes of bad workmen, is answerable to themselves and animating to feeble Artistes. I, therefore, secure of your Honors Clemencie, and herein not unlike to* Phaëton *(who at the first did fearefully admire even the Pallace of* Phœbus, *but anon feareles adventure even the presence of* Phœbus) *having dedicated a former Booke to him that from your Honor deriveth his Birth, now secondly present the like to your Lordship: with so much the lesse doubt, and so much the more dutie, by how much the more I esteeme this my latter labour of more valew, and (omitting your high Titles) I owe, and your Lordship expecteth especiall duetie at the hands of your Servaunt. And thus (right Honorable) hoping better than I can performe, and yet fearing lesser than I may offend, desirous to please, desperate of praise, & destitute of a better Present, I make tender only of good will: more I have not, for your Honors good worde, lesse I hope not.*

Your Lordships most humble and
duetifull Servant, *W. Warner.*

William Byrd, *Psalmes, Sonnets, and Songs of Sadness and Piety,* 1588.

The Epistle to the Reader.

BENIGNE Reader, heere is offered unto thy courteous acceptation, Musicke of sundrie sorts, and to content divers humors. If thou bee disposed to pray, heere are *Psalmes;* if to bee merrie, heere are *Sonets;* if to lament for thy sins, heere are songs of sadnesse and *Pietie.* If thou delight in Musicke of great compasse, heere are divers songs, which beeing originally made for Instruments to expresse the harmony, and one voyce to pronounce the dittie, are now framed in all parts for voyces to sing the same. If thou desire songs of smal compasse and fit for the reach of most voyces, heere are most in number of that sort. Whatsoever paines I have taken heerein, I shall thinke to be well imployed, if the same bee well accepted, Musicke thereby the better loved, and the more exercised. In the expressing of these songs, either by voyces or Instruments, if there happen to bee any jarre or dissonance, blame not the Printer, who (I doe assure thee) through his great paines and diligence, doth heere deliver to thee a perfect and true Coppie. If in the composition of these Songs, there bee any fault by mee committed, I desire the skilfull, eyther with courtesie to let the same bee concealed, or in friendly sort to bee thereof admonished: and at the next Impression he shall finde the error reformed: remembring alwaies, that it is more easie to finde a fault then to amend it. If thou finde any thing heere worthie of liking and commendation, give praise unto God, from whom (as from a most pure and plentifull fountaine) all good guiftes of Sciences dooe flow: whose name bee glorified for ever.

The most assured friend to all
that love or learne Musicke:
William Byrd.

Sir Philip Sidney, *Arcadia*, 1590.

TO MY DEARE LADIE AND SISTER, THE COUN TESSE OF PEMBROKE.

HERE *now have you (most deare, and most worthy to be most deare Lady) this idle worke of mine: which I fear (like the Spiders webbe) will be thought fitter to be swept away, then worn to any other purpose. For my part, in very trueth (as the cruell fathers among the Greekes, were woont to doo to the babes they would not foster) I could well find in my harte, to cast out in some desert of forgetfulnes this child which I am loath to father. But you desired me to doo it, and your desire, to my hart is an absolute commandement. Now, it is done onelie for you, onely to you; if you keepe it to your selfe, or to such friendes, who will weigh errors in the ballaunce of good will, I hope, for the fathers sake, it will be pardoned, perchance made much of, though in it selfe it have deformities. For indeede, for severer eyes it is not, being but a trifle, and that triflinglie handled. Your deare selfe can best witnes the maner, being done in loose sheetes of paper, most of it in your presence, the rest, by sheetes, sent unto you, as fast as they were done. In summe, a young head, not so well stayed as I would it were, (and shall be when God will) having many many fancies begotten in it, if it had not ben in some way delivered, would have growen a monster, & more sorie might I be that they came in, then that they gat out. But his chiefe safetie, shalbe the not walking abroad; & his chiefe protection, the bearing the liverye of your name; which (if much much good will do not deceave me) is worthy to be a sanctuary for a greater offender. This say I, because I knowe the vertue so; and this say I, because it may be ever so; or to say better, because it will be ever so. Read it then at your idle tymes, and the follyes your good judgement wil finde in it, blame not, but laugh at. And so, looking for no better stuffe, then, as in an Haberdashers shoppe, glasses, or feathers, you will continue to love the writer, who doth excedinglie love you, and most hartelie praies you may long live to be a principall ornament to the familie of the* Sidneis.

Your loving Brother
Philip Sidnei.

Thomas Watson, *Melibœus,* 1590.

To the courteous Reader.

GENTLEMEN, if you suppose me vaine for translating myne owne poeme, or negligent, for not doing it exactly to the latin originall, I thus desire to satisfie you. It is pardonable for a man to be bold with his owne; and I interpret my self, lest Melibaeus in speaking English by an other mans labour, should leefe my name in his chaunge, as my *Amyntas* did. A third fault (haply) will bee found, that my pastorall discourse to the unlearned may seeme obscure: which to prevent, I have thought good here to advertise you, that I figure Englande in *Arcadia;* Her Majestie in *Diana;* Sir Francis Walsingham in *Melibaeus,* and his Ladie in *Dryas;* Sir Phillippe Sidney in *Astrophill,* and his Ladie in *Hyale,* Master Thomas Walsingham in *Tyterus,* and my selfe in *Corydon.*

Desirous to please you
Tho. Watson.

Giles Fletcher, *Of the Russe Common Wealth,* 1591.

To the Queenes most ex-*cellent Majestie.*

MOST gracious Soveraigne, beeyng employed in your Majesties service to the Emperour of *Russia,* I observed the State, and manners of that Countrey. And having reduced the same into some order, by the way as I returned, I have presumed to offer it in this smal Booke to your most excellent Majestie. My meaning was to note thinges for mine owne experience, of more importaunce then delight, and rather true then strange. In their maner of government, your Highnesse may see both: A true and strange face of a *Tyrannical state,* most unlike to your own, without true knowledge of GOD, without written Lawe, without common justice: save that which proceedeth from their *Speaking Lawe,* to wit, the Magistrate who hath most neede of a Lawe, to restraine his owne injustice. The practise hereof as it is heavy, and grievous to the poore oppressed people that live within those Countreyes: so it may give just cause to my selfe, and other your Majesties faithfull subjects, to acknowledge our happines on this behalfe, and give God thankes for your Majesties most Princelike, and gracious government: as also to your Highnesse more joy, and contentment in your royall estate, in that you are a Prince of subjectes, not of slaves, that are kept within duetie by love, not by feare. The Almightie stil blesse your Highnese with a most long, and happy reigne in this life, and with Christ Jesus in the life to come.

Your majesties most humble
subject, and servant,
G. Fletcher.

John Lyly, *Endimion*, 1591.

The Printer to the *Reader.*

SINCE the Plaies in Paules were dissolved, there are certaine Commedies come to my handes by chaunce, which were presented before her Majestie at severall times by the children of Paules. This is the first, and if in any place it shall dysplease, I will take more paines to perfect the next. I referre it to thy indifferent judgement to peruse, whom I woulde willinglie please. And if this may passe with thy good lyking, I will then goe forwarde to publish the rest. In the meane time, let this have thy good worde for my better encouragement.

Farewell.

Sir Philip Sidney, *Astrophel and Stella,* 1591.

Somewhat to reade for them *that list.*

TEMPUS *adest plausus; aurea pompa venit:* so endes the Sceane of Idiots, and enter *Astrophel* in pompe. Gentlemen that have seene a thousand lines of folly drawn forth *ex uno puncto impudentiæ* & two famous Mountains to goe to the conception of one Mouse, that have had your eares deafned with the eccho of Fames brasen towres when only they have been toucht with a leaden pen, that have seene *Pan* sitting in his bower of delights & a number of *Midasses* to admire his miserable hornepipes, let not your surfeted sight, new come from such puppet play, think scorne to turn aside into this Theater of pleasure, for here you shal find a paper stage streud with pearle, an artificial heav'n to overshadow the faire frame, & christal wals to encounter your curious eyes, while the tragicommody of love is performed by starlight. The chiefe Actor here is *Melpomene,* whose dusky robes, dipt in the inke of teares, as yet seeme to drop when I view them neere. The argument cruell chastitie, the Prologue hope, the Epilogue dispaire; *videte, quaeso, et linguis animisque favete.* And here, peradventure, my witles youth may be taxt with a margent note of presumption for offering to put up any motion of applause in the behalfe of so excellent a Poet (the least sillable of whose name sounded in the eares of judgement, is able to give the meanest line he writes a dowry of immortality); yet those that observe how jewels oftentimes com to their hands that know not their value, & that the cockscombes of our daies, like *Esops* Cock, had rather have a Barly kernell wrapt up in a Ballet then they wil dig for the welth of wit in any ground that they know not, I hope wil also hold me excused though I open the gate to his glory & invite idle eares to the admiration of his melancholy.

Quid petitur sacris nisi tantum fama poetis?

Which although it be oftentimes imprisoned in Ladyes casks & the president bookes of such as cannot see without another mans spectacles, yet at length it breakes foorth in spight of his keepers, and useth some private penne (in steed of a picklock) to procure his violent enlargement.

The Sunne for a time may maske his golden head in a cloud, yet in the end, the thicke vaile doth vanish, and his embellished blandishment appeares. Long hath *Astrophel* (Englands Sunne) withheld the beames of his spirite from the common view of our darke sence, and night hath hovered over the gardens of the nine Sisters, while *Ignis fatuus* and grosse fatty flames (such as commonly arise out of Dunghilles) have tooke occasion, in the middest eclipse of his shining perfections, to wander a broade with a wispe of paper at their tailes like Hobgoblins, and leade men up and downe in a circle of absurditie a whole weeke, and never know where they are. But nowe that cloude of sorrow is dissolved which fierie Love exhaled from his dewie haire, and affection hath unburthened the labouring streames of her wombe in the lowe cesterne of his grave; the night hath resigned her jettie throne unto *Lucifer,* and cleere daylight possesseth the skie that was dimmed; wherfore breake off your daunce, you Fayries and Elves, and from the fieldes with the torne carcases of your Timbrils, for your kingdome is expired. Put out your rush candles, you Poets and Rimers, and bequeath your crazed quaterzayns to the Chaundlers; for loe, here he commeth that hath broekn your legs. *Apollo* hath resigned his Ivory Harp unto *Astrophel,* & he, like *Mercury,* must lull you a sleep with his musicke. Sleepe *Argus,* sleep Ignorance, sleep Impudence, for *Mercury* hath *Io,* & onely *Io Pæan* belongeth to *Astrophel.* Deare *Astrophel,* that in the ashes of thy Love livest againe like the *Phœnix,* O might thy bodie (as thy name) live againe likewise here amongst us! but the earth, the mother of mortalitie, hath snacht thee too soone into her chilled colde armes, and will not let thee by any meanes be drawne from her deadly imbrace; and thy divine Soule, carried on an Angels wings to heaven, is installed in *Hermes* place, sole *prolocutor* to the Gods. Therefore mayest thou never returne from the *Elisian* fieldes like *Orpheus;* therefore must we ever mourne for our *Orpheus.*

Fayne would a seconde spring of passion heere spende it selfe on his sweet remembrance; but Religion, that rebuketh prophane lamentation, drinkes in the rivers of those dispaireful teares which languorous ruth hath outwelled, & bids me looke back to the house of honor, where from one and the selfe same roote of renowne, I shal find many goodly branches derived, & such as, with the spreading increase of their vertues, may somwhat overshadow the griefe of his los. Amongst the which, fayre sister of *Phœbus,* & eloquent secretary to the Muses, most rare Countesse of *Pembroke,* thou art not to be omitted, whom Artes doe adore as a second *Minerva,* and our Poets extoll as the Patronesse of their invention; for in thee the *Lesbian Sappho* with her lirick Harpe is disgraced, & the Laurel Garlande which thy Brother so bravely advaunst on his Launce is still kept greene in the Temple of *Pallas*. Thou only sacrificest thy soule to contemplation, thou only entertainest emptie handed *Homer*, & keepest the springs of *Castalia* from being dryed up. Learning, wisedom, beautie, and all other ornaments of Nobilitie whatsoever seeke to approve themselves in thy sight, and get a further seale of felicity from the smiles of thy favour:

O Jove digna viro ni Jove nata fores.

I feare I shall be counted a mercenary flatterer for mixing my thoughts with such figurative admiration, but generall report that surpasseth my praise condemneth my rethoricke of dulnesse for so colde a commendation. Indeede, to say the truth, my stile is somewhat heavie gated, and cannot daunce, trip, and goe so lively, with oh! my love, ah! my love, all my loves gone, as other Sheepheards that have beene fooles in the Morris time out of minde; nor hath my prose any skill to imitate the Almond leape verse, or sit tabring five yeres together nothing but to bee, to hee, on a paper drum. Onely I can keepe pace with Gravesend barge, and care not if I have water enough to lande my ship of fooles with the Tearme (the tyde I shoulde say). Now every man is not of that minde; for some, to goe the lighter away, will take in their fraught of spangled feathers, golden Peebles, Straw, Reedes, Bulrushes, or any thing, and then they beare out their sayles as proudly as if they were balisted with Bulbiefe. Others are so hardly bested for loading that they are faine to retaile the cinders of *Troy*, and the shivers of broken trunchions, to fill up their boate that else should goe empty; and if they have but a pound weight of good Merchandise, it shall be placed at the poope, or pluckt in a thousande peeces to credit their carriage. For my part, every man as he likes, *Mens cuiusque is est quisque*. 'Tis as good to goe in cut fingerd Pumps as corke shooes, if one were Cornish diamonds on his toes. To explain it by a more familiar example, an Asse is no great statesman in the beastes common-wealth, though he weare his eares *upsevant muffe,* after the Muscovy fashion, & hange the lip like a Capcase halfe open, or look as demurely as a sixpenny browne loafe, for he hath some imperfections that do keepe him from the common Councel; yet of many he is deemed a very vertuous member, and one of the honestest sort of men that are. So that our opinion (as *Sextus Empedocus* affirmeth) gives the name of good or ill to every thing. Out of whose works (latelie translated into English, for the benefit of unlearned writers) a man might collect a whole booke of this argument, which no doubt woulde prove a worthy commonwealth matter, and far better than wits waxe karnell: much good worship have the Author.

Such is this golden age wherein we live, and so replenisht with golden Asses of all sortes, that, if learning had lost it selfe in a grove of Genealogies, wee neede doe no more but sette an olde goose over halfe a dozen pottle pots (which are as it were the egges of invention), and wee shall have such a breede of bookes within a little while after, as will fill all the world with the wilde fowle of good wits. I can tell you this is a harder thing then making golde of quicksilver, and will trouble you more then the Morrall of *Æsops* Glow-worme hath troubled our English Apes, who, striving to warme themselves with the flame of the Philosophers stone, have spent all their wealth in buying bellowes to blowe this false fyre. Gentlemen, I feare I have too much presumed on your idle leysure, and beene too bold to stand talking all this while in an other mans doore; but now I will leave you to survey the pleasures of *Paphos,* and offer your smiles on the Aulters of *Venus*.

Yours in all desire to please,

Tho: Nashe.

Robert Wilmot, *Tancred and Gismund*, 1591.

TO THE WORSHIPFULL AND *learned Societie, the Gentlemen Students of the Inner Temple, with the rest of his singular good friends, the Gentlemen of the middle Temple, and to all other curteous readers,* R.W. *wisheth increase of all health, worship & learning, with the immortall glorie of the graces adorning the same.*

YE may perceive (right Worshipful) in perusing the former Epistle sent to mee, how sore I am beset with the importunities of my friends, to publish this Pamphlet. Truly I am and have bin (if there be in me anie soundnes of judgement) of this opinion, that whatsoever is committed to the presse is commended to eternitie, and it shall stand a lively witnes with our conscience, to our comfort or confusion, in the reckning of that great daie.

Advisedly therefore was that Proverbe used of our elder Philosophers, *Manum a Tabula:* with-hold thy hand from the paper, and thy papers from the print or light of the world; for a lewd word escaped is irrevocable, but a bad or base discourse published in print is intollerable.

Hereupon I have indured some conflicts between reason and judgement, whether it were convenient for the commonwealth, with the *indecorum* of my calling (as some thinke it) that the memorie of *Tancreds* Tragedie should be againe by my meanes, revived, which the oftner I read over, and the more I considered theron, the sooner I was won to consent therunto: calling to mind that neither the thrice reverend & lerned father M. Beza, was ashamed in his yonger yeres, to send abroad in his owne name, his Tragedy of *Abraham,* nor that rare Scot (the scholer of our age) *Buchanan,* his most pathetical *Jeptha.*

Indeed I must willingly confesse this worke simple, and not worth comparison to any of theirs for the writers of them were grave men; of this, young heads. In them is shewn the perfection of their studies; in this, the imperfection of their wits. Neverthe-les herein they al agree, commending vertue, detesting vice, and lively deciphering their overthrow that suppresse not their un-ruely affections. These things noted herin, how simple so ever the verse be, I hope the matter wil be acceptable to the wise.

Wherefore I am now bold to present *Gismund* to your sights, and unto yours only, for therfore have I conjured her, by the love that hath bin these 24. yeres betwixt us, that she waxe not so proude of her fresh painting, to stragle in her plumes abroad, but to contein her selfe within the walles of your house; so am I sure she shal be safe from the *Tragedian Tyrants* of our time, who are not ashamed to affirme that ther can no amarous poeme savour of any sharpnes of wit, unlesse it be seasoned with scurrilous words.

But leaving them to their lewdnes, I hope you & all discreet readers wil thankfully receive my pains, the fruites of my first harvest: the rather, perceiving that my purpose in this Tragedie tendeth onely to the exaltation of vertue & suppression of vice, with pleasure to profit and help al men, but to offend or hurt no man. As for such as have neither the grace, nor the good gift to doe well themselves, nor the common honestie to speak wel of others, I must (as I may) heare and bear their baitings with patience.

Yours devoted in his ability, *R. Wilmot.*

Robert Greene, *Greenes Groatsworth of Wit*, 1592.

The Printer to the Gentle Readers.

I HAVE published here Gentlemen for your mirth and benefite, *Greenes Groates Worth of Wit.* With sundry of his pleasant discourses, ye have beene before delighted. But nowe hath death given a period to his pen, onely this happened into my handes which I have published for your pleasures. Accept it favourably because it was his last birth and not least worth, in my poore opinion. But I will cease to praise that which is above my conceipt, & leave it selfe to speak for it selfe: and so abide your learned censuring.

Yours W. W.

Robert Greene, *Greenes Groatsworth of Wit,* 1592.

To the Gentlemen Readers.

GENTLEMEN. *The Swan sings melodiously before death, that in all his life time useth but a jarring sound.* Greene *though able inough to write, yet deeplyer serched with sicknes than ever heeretofore, sendes you his Swanne-like songe for that he feares he shall never againe carroll to you woonted love layes, never againe discover to you youths pleasures. How ever yet sicknesse, riot, incontinence, have at once shown their extremitie; yet if I recover, you shall all see more fresh sprigs then ever sprang from me, directing you how to live, yet not diswading ye from love. This is the last I have writ, and I feare me the last I shall writ. And how ever I have beene censured for some of my former bookes, yet Gentlemen I protest they were as I had speciall information. But passing them, I commend this to your favourable censures, that like an Embrion without shape, I feare me will be thrust into the world. If I live to end it, it shall be otherwise: if not, yet will I commend it to your courtesies, that you may as well be acquainted with my repentant death, as you have lamented my careles course of life. But as* Nemo ante obitum felix, *so* Acta Exitus probat: *Beseeching therefore so to be deemed heereof as I deserve, I leave the worke to your likinges, and leave you to your delightes.*

Robert Greene, *Greenes Groatsworth of Wit,* 1592.

To those Gentlemen his Quondam acquaintance, that spend their wits in making plaies, R. G. wisheth a better exercise, and wisdome to prevent his extremities.

IF wofull experience may move you (Gentlemen) to beware, or unheard of wretchednes intreate you to take heed, I doubt not but you wil looke backe with sorrow on your time past, and indevour with repentance to spend that which is to come. Wonder not (for with thee wil I first begin) thou famous gracer of Tragedians, that *Greene,* who hath said with thee (like the foole in his heart) There is no God, shoulde now give glorie unto his greatnes: for penetrating is his power, his hand lyes heavie upon me, hee hath spoken unto mee with a voice of thunder, and I have felt he is a God that can punish enemies. Why should thy excellent wit, his gift, bee so blinded, that thou shouldst give no glorie to the giver? Is it pestilent Machivilian pollicy that thou hast studied? O peevish follie! What are his rules but meere confused mockeries, able to extirpate in small time the generation of mankind? For if *Sic volo, sic jubeo,* hold in those that are able to commaund: and if it be lawfull *Fas & nefas* to do any thing that is beneficiall, onely Tyrants should possesse the earth, and they striving to exceed in tyrannie, should each to other be a slaughter man: till the mightiest outliving all, one stroke were lefte for

Death, that in one age mans life should end. The brother of this Diabolicall Atheisme is dead, and in his life had never the felicitie hee aymed at: but as he began in craft, lived in feare, and ended in despaire. *Quàm inscrutabilia sunt Dei judicia?* This murderer of many brethren, had his conscience feared like *Caine:* this betrayer of him that gave his life for him, inherited the portion of *Judas:* this Apostata perished as ill as *Julian:* and wilt thou my friend be his disciple? Looke but to me, by him perswaded to that libertie, and thou shalt find it an infernall bondage. I knowe the least of my demerits merit this miserable death, but wilfull striving against knowne truth, exceedeth all the terrors of my soule. Defer not (with me) till this last point of extremitie; for litle knowst thou how in the end thou shalt be visited.

With thee I joyne yong *Juvenall,* that byting Satyrist, that lastly with mee together writ a Comedie. Sweet boy, might I advise thee, be advisde, and get not many enemies by bitter wordes: inveigh against vaine men, for thou canst do it, no man better, no man so well: thou hast a libertie to reproove all, and name none; for one being spoken to, all are offended, none being blamed no man is injured. Stop shallow water still running, it will rage, or tread on a worme and it will turne: then blame not Schollers vexed with sharpe lines, if they reprove thy too much liberty of reproofe.

And thou no lesse deserving than the other two, in some things rarer, in nothing inferiour; driven (as my selfe) to extreme shifts, a litle have I to say to thee: and were it not an idolatrous oth, I would sweare by sweet *S. George,* thou art unworthy better hap, sith thou dependest on so meane a stay. Base minded men all three of you, if by my miserie you be not warnd: for unto none of you (like mee) sought those burres to cleave: those Puppets (I meane) that spake from our mouths, those Anticks garnisht in our colours. Is it not strange that I, to whom they all have beene beholding: is it not like that you, to whome they all have beene beholding, shall (were yee in that case as I am now) bee both at once of them forsaken? Yes, trust them not: for there is an upstart Crow, beautified with our feathers, that with his *Tygers hart wrapt in a Players hyde,* supposes he is as well able to bombast out a blanke verse as the best of you: and beeing an absolute *Johannes fac totum,* is in his owne conceit the onely Shake-scene in a countrey. O that I might intreat your rare wits to be imployed in more profitable courses: & let those Apes imitate your past excellence, and never more acquaint them with your admired inventions. I knowe the best husband of you all will never prove an Usurer, and the kindest of them all will never prove a kind nurse. Yet whilest you may, seeke you better Maisters; for it is pittie men of such rare wits, should be subject to the pleasure of such rude groomes.

In this I might insert two more, that both have writ against these buckram Gentlemen: but lette their owne workes serve to witnesse against their owne wickednesse, if they persevere to maintaine any more such peasants. For other new-commers, I leave them to the mercie of these painted monsters, who (I doubt not) will drive the best minded to despise them: for the rest, it skils not though they make a jeast at them.

But now returne I againe to you three, knowing my miserie is to you no newes; and let mee hartily intreat you to be warned by my harms. Delight not (as I have done) in irreligious oathes; for from the blasphemers house, a curse shall not depart. Despise drunkennes which wasteth the wit and maketh men all equall unto beasts. Flie lust, as the deathsman of the soule, and defile not the Temple of the holy Ghost. Abhorre those Epicures whose loose life hath made religion lothsome to your eares; and when they sooth you with tearms of Maistership, remember *Robert Greene,* whome they have often so flattered, perishes now for want of comfort. Remember Gentlemen, your lives are like so many lighted Tapers, that are with care delivered to all of you to maintaine: these with wind-puft wrath may be extinguisht, which drunkennes put out, which negligence let fall: for mans time is not of it selfe so short, but it is more shortned by sinne. The fire of my light is now at the last snuffe, and for want of wherewith to sustaine it, there is no substance lefte for life to feede on. Trust not then (I beseech ye) to such weake staies: for they are as changeable in minde, as in many attyres. Wel, my hand is tyrde, and I am forst to leave where I would begin; for a whole booke cannot containe their wrongs, which I am forst to knit up in some fewe lines of words.

Desirous that you should live,
though himselfe be dying:
Robert Greene.

Robert Greene, *Greenes Groatsworth of Wit,* 1592.

A letter writen to his wife, founde with this booke after his death.

THE remembrance of the many wrongs offred thee and thy unreproved vertues adde greater sorrow to my miserable state than I can utter or thou conceive. Neither is it lessened by consideration of thy absence (though shame would hardly let me behold thy face) but exceedingly aggravated, for that I cannot (as I ought) to thy owne selfe reconcile my selfe, that thou mightst witnes my inward woe at this instant, that have made thee a wofull wife for so long a time. But equall heaven hath denide that comfort, giving at my last neede like succour as I have sought all my life: being in this extremitie as voide of helpe, as thou hast beene of hope. Reason would, that after so long wast, I should not send thee a child to bring thee greater charge; but consider, he is the fruit of thy wombe, in whose face regarde not the Fathers faults so much, as thy owne perfections. He is yet Greene, and may grow straight, if he be carefully tended: otherwise, apt enough (I feare mee) to follow his Fathers folly. That I have offended thee highly I knowe, that thou canst forget my injuries I hardly beleeve: yet perswade I my selfe, if thou saw my wretched estate, thou couldst not but lament it: nay, certainly I know thou wouldst. All my wrongs muster themselves before mee, every evill at once plagues mee. For my contempt of

God, I am contemned of men: for my swearing and forswearing, no man will beleeve me: for my gluttony, I suffer hunger: for my drunkennes, thirst: for my adultery, ulcerous sores. Thus God hath cast me downe, that I might be humbled: and punished me for example of other sinners: and although he strangely suffers me in this world to perish without succor, yet trust I in the world to come to find mercie, by the merites of my Saviour, to whom I commend thee, and commit my soule.

Thy repentant husband for his disloyaltie, Robert Greene.

Fælicem fuisse infaustum.

Henry Chettle, *Kind-Hartes Dreame,* 1592.

To the Gentlemen Readers.

IT hath beene a custome, Gentlemen, (in my mind commendable) among former Authors (whose workes are no lesse beautified with eloquente phrase than garnished with excellent example) to begin an exordium to the Readers of their time; much more convenient, I take it, should the writers in these daies (wherein that gravitie of enditing, by the elder excercised, is not observ'd, nor that modest decorum kept which they continued) submit their labours to the favourable censures of their learned overseers. For, seeing nothing can be said that hath not been before said, the singularitie of some mens conceits (otherwayes exellent well deserving) are no more to be soothed, than the peremptorie posies of two very sufficient Translators commended. To come in print is not to seeke praise but to crave pardon. I am urgd to the one, and bold to begge the other; he that offendes, being forst, is more excusable than the wilfull faultie; though both be guilty, there is difference in the guilt. To observe custome, and avoid as I may, cavill, opposing your favors against my feare, Ile shew reason for my present writing, and after proceed to sue for pardon. About three moneths since died M. Robert Greene, *leaving many papers in sundry Booke sellers hands, among other his Groats-worth of wit, in which, a letter written to divers play-makers, is offensively by one or two of them taken, and because on the dead they cannot be avenged, they wilfully forge in their conceites a living Author: and after tossing it two and fro, no remedy, but it must light on me. How I have, all the time of my conversing in printing, hindred the bitter inveying against schollers, it hath been very well knowne, and how in that I dealt I can sufficiently proove. With neither of them that take offence was I acquainted, and with one of them I care not if I never be. The other, whome at that time I did not so much spare, as since I wish I had, for that as I have moderated the heate of living writers, and might have usde my owne discretion (especially in such a case) the Author beeing dead, that I did not, I am as sory, as if the originall fault had beene my fault, because my selfe have seene his demeanor no lesse civill than he exclent in the qualitie he professes. Besides, divers of worship have reported his uprightnes of dealing, which argues his honesty, and his facetious grace in writting, that aprooves his Art. For the first, whose learning I reverence, and, at the perusing of* Greenes *Booke, stroke out what then, in conscience I thought, he in some displeasure writ: or had it beene true, yet to publish it was intollerable: him I would wish to use me no worse than I deserve. I had onely in the copy this share, it was il written, as sometime* Greenes *hand was none of the best, licensd it must be, ere it could bee printed, which could never be if it might not be read. To be breife, I writ it over, and, as neare as I could, followed the copy, onely in that letter I put something out, but in the whole booke not a worde in, for I protest it was all* Greenes, *not mine nor Maister* Nashes, *as some unjustly have affirmed. Neither was he the writer of an Epistle to the second part of Gerileon, though, by the workemans error, T. N. were set to the end. That I confesse to be mine, and repent it not.*

Thus, Gentlemen, having noted the private causes that made me nominate my selfe in print; being, as well to purge Master Nashe *of that he did not, as to justifie what I did, and withall to confirme what M.* Greene *did: I beseech yee accept the publike cause, which is both the desire of your delight and common benefite: for, though the toye bee shadowed under the Title of* Kind-hearts Dreame, *it discovers the false hearts of divers that wake to commit mischiefe. Had not the former reasons been, it had come forth without a father: and then shuld I have had no cause to feare offending, or reason to sue for favour. Now am I in doubt of the one, though I hope of the other; which if I obtaine, you shall bind me hereafter to bee silent till I can present yee with some thing more acceptable.*

Henrie Chettle.

Henry Chettle, *Kind-Hartes Dreame,* 1592.

Kind-Hartes Dedication of his dreame, to all the pleasant conceited whersoever.

GENTLEMEN and good-fellowes (whose kindnes having christened mee with the name of Kind-heart bindes me in all kind course I can to deserve the continuance of your love) let it not seeme strange (I beseech ye) that he, that all daies of his life hath beene famous for drawing teeth, should now, in drooping age, hazard contemptible infamie by drawing himselfe into print. For such is the folly of this age, so witlesse, so audacious, that there are scarce so manye pedlers brag themselves to be printers because they have a bundel of ballads in their packe, as there be idiots that thinke themselves Artists because they can English an obligation, or write a true staffe to the tune of fortune. This folly, raging universally, hath infired me to write the remembrance of sundry of my deceased frends, personages not alltogether obscure, for then were my subject base, nor yet of any honourable carriage, for my stile is rude and bad: and, to such as I, it belongs not to jest with Gods. Kind-hart would have his companions esteeme of Estates as starres, on whom meane men maye looke, but not over-looke. I have heard of an eloquent Orator, that trimly furnished with warres abiliments, had on his shield this motto, *Bona fortuna:* yet, at the first meeting of the enimy, fled without fight. For which being reprooved, he replied;

If I have saved my selfe in this battell by flight, I shall live to chase the enimy in the next. So, Gentlemen, fares it with mee. If envious misconsterers arme themselves against my simple meaning, and wrest every jest to a wrong sense, I thinke it policy to fly at the first fight, till I gather fresh forces to represse their folly. Neither can they, what ever they be, deale hardly with Kind-hart, for he onely delivers his dreame, with every Apparition simply as it was uttered. Its fond for them to fight against ghosts: its fearefull for me to hide an Apparition: by concealing it I might doe my selfe harme and them no good; by revealing it ease my hart and doe no honest men hurt: for the rest (although I would not willingy move the meanest) they must beare as I doe, or mend it as they may. Well, least ye deeme all my dreame but an Epistle, I will proceed to that without any further circumstance.

Henry Constable, *Diana*, 1592.

THE PRINTER TO the Reader.

OBSCUR'D wonders (gentlemen) visited me in *Turnus* armor, and I in regard of *Aeneas* honour, have unclouded them unto the worlde. You are that Universe, you that *Aeneas*. If you finde *Pallas* gyrdle, murder them, if not inviron'd with barbarizme, save them, and eternitie will prayse you.

Vale.

Samuel Daniel, *Delia,* 1592.

TO THE RIGHT HO-nourable the Ladie *Mary,* Countesse of Pembroke.

R*IGHT honorable, although I rather desired to keep in the private passions of my youth from the multitude as things utterd to my selfe and consecrated to silence, yet seeing I was betraide by the indiscretion of a greedie Printer and had some of my secrets bewraide to the world uncorrected, doubting the like of the rest, I am forced to publish that which I never ment. But this wrong was not onely doone to mee, but to him whose unmatchable lines have indured the like misfortune, ignorance sparing not to commit sacriledge upon so holy Reliques. Yet* Astrophel *flying with the wings of his own fame a higher pitch then the gross-sighted can discerne hath registred his owne name in the Annals of eternitie, and cannot be disgraced, howsoever disguised. And for my selfe, seeing I am thrust out into the worlde, and that my unboldned Muse is forced to appeare so rawly in publique, I desire onely to bee graced by the countenance of your protection: whome the fortune of our time hath made the happie and judiciall Patronesse of the Muses (a glory hereditary to your house) to preserve them from those hidious Beastes, Oblivion and Barbarisme, wherbey you doe not onely possesse the honour of the present but also do bind posterity to an ever gratefull memorie* *of your vertues, wherein you must survive your selfe. And if my lines heereafter, better laboured, shall purchase grace in the world, they must remaine the monuments of your honourable favour, and recorde the zealous duetie of mee, who am vowed to your honour in all observancy for ever,*

Samuel Danyell.

Barnabe Barnes, *Parthenophil and Parthenope*, 1593.

To the Learned Gentlemen Readers The Printer.

GENTLEMEN. These laboures followinge, beeinge come of late into my handes barely, without title or subscription; partly moved by certain of my deere friends, but especially by the worth & excellency of the worke, I thought it well deserving my labour, to participate them to your judiciall viewes: where, both for variety of conceites, and sweete Poesie, you shall doubtlesse finde that which shall be most commendable, and woorth your readinge. The Author, though at the first unknowne (yet enforced to accorde to certaine of his friendes importunacy herein, to publish them, by their meanes, and for their sakes) [is] unwilling, as it seemeth, to acknowledge them, for their levity, till he have redeemed them, with some more excellent worke hereafter. Till when, he requesteth your favorable and indifferent censures of these his over youthfull Poemes, submitting them to your friendly patronages.

Farewell, this of May, 1593.

Giles Fletcher (the elder), *Licia*, 1593.

To the Reader.

I HAD thought (curteous and gentle Reader) not to have troubled thy patience with these lines; but that, in the neglect thereof, I shoulde either scorne thee, as careless of thine opinion (a thing savouring of a proud humour) or dispaire to obtaine thy favor, which I am loth to conceive of thy good nature. If I were knowne, I would intreat in the best manner, and speake for him whome thou knewest. But beeing not knowne, thou speakest not against me; and therefore I much care not. For this kinde of poetrie wherein I wrote, I did it onelie to trie my humour. And for the matter of love, it may bee I am so devoted to some one into whose hands these may light by chance, that she may say, which thou nowe sayest (that surelie he is in love) which if she doe, then have I the full recompence of my labour; and the Poems have dealt sufficientlie for the discharge of their owne duetie. This age is learnedlie wise, and faultles in this kind of making their wittes knowne: thinking so baselie of our bare English (wherein thousandes have traveilled with such ill lucke) that they deeme themselves barbarous and the Iland barren, unlesse they have borrowed from Italie, Spaine, *and* France *their best and choicest conceites. For my owne parte, I am of this mind that our nation is so exquisite (neither woulde I overweininglie seeme to flatter our home-spunne stuffe, or diminish the credite of our brave traveilers) that neither* Italie, Spaine, *nor* France *can goe beyond us for exact invention. For if anie thing be odious amongst us, it is the exile of our olde maners, and some base-borne phrases stuft up with such newe tearmes as a man may sooner feele us to flatter by our incrouching eloquence than suspect it from the eare. And for the matter of love, where everie man takes upon him to court exactlie, I could justlie grace (if it be a grace to be excllent in that kinde) the Innes of Court, and some Gentlemen like[wise] students in both Universities, whose learning and bringing up together with their fine natures makes so sweet a harmonie as, without partialitie, the most injurious will preferre them before all others; and therefore they onelie are fittest to write of Love. For others, for the moste parte, are men of meane reach, whose imbased mindes praie uppon everie badde dish: men unfitte to knowe what love meanes; deluded fondlie with their owne conceit, misdeeming so divine a fancie; taking it to bee the contentment of themselves, the shame of others, the wrong of vertue, and the refiner of the tongue, boasting of some fewe favours. These and such like errours (errours hatefull to an upright minde) commonlie by learnlesse heades are reputed for loves kingdome. But vaine men, naturallie led, deluded themselves, deceive others. For* Love *is a Goddesse (pardon me though I speake like a Poet) not respecting the contentment of him that loves but the vertues of the beloved, satisfied with woondering, fedde with admiration, respecting nothing but his Ladies woorthinesse, made as happie by love as by all favours, chaste by honour, farre from violence: respecting but one; and that one in such kindnesse, honestie, trueth, constancie, and honour, as were all the world offered to make a change, yet the boote were too small, and therefore bootles. This is love, and farre more than this; which I knowe a vulgare head, a base minde, an ordinarie conceit, a common person will not, nor cannot have. Thus doe I commende that love wherewith, in these poemes, I have honoured the worthie* LICIA. *But the love wherewith* Venus sonne *hath injuriouslie made spoile of thousandes, is a cruell tyrant: occasion of sighes, oracle of lies, enemie of pittie, way of errour, shape of inconstancie, temple of treason, faith without assurance, monarch of tears, murtherer of ease, prison of heartes, monster of nature, poisoned honney, impudant courtizan, furious bastard: and in one word, not* Love. *Thus, Reader, take heede thou erre not! Esteeme* Love *as thou ought. If thou muse what my* LICIA *is, take her to be some* Diana, *at the least chaste, or some* Minerva, *no* Venus, *fairer farre. It may be shee is Learnings image, or some heavenlie woonder: which the precisest may not mislike. Perhaps under that name I have shadowed* Discipline. *It may be, I meane that kinde courtesie which I found at the Patronesse of these Poems, it may bee some Colledge. It may bee my conceit, and portende nothing. Whatsoever it be, if thou like it, take it! and thanke the worthie Ladie* MOLLINEUX, *for whose sake thou hast it: worthie indeed, and so not onlie reputed by me in private affection of thankefulnesse, but so equallie to be esteemed by all that knowe her. For if I had not received of her and good* Sir RICHARD, *of kind and wise* M. LEE, *of curteous* M. HOUGHTON, *all matchlesse, matched in one kindred, those unrequitable favours, I had not thus idlely toyed. If thou mislike it, yet she, or they, or both, or divine* LICIA *shall patronize it: or if none, I will, and can, doe it my selfe. Yet I wish thy favour. Do but say, Thou art content; and I rest thine. If not, farewel, till we both meete. Septemb. 8. 1593.*

Thomas Nashe, *Christ's Teares over Jerusalem,* 1593.

To the Reader.

NIL *nisi flere libet,* Gentles, heere is no joyfull subject towardes, if you will weepe, so it is. I have nothing to spend on you but passion. A hundred unfortunate farewels to fantasticall Satirisme. In those vaines heere-to-fore have I mispent my spirite, and prodigally conspir'd against good houres. Nothing is there nowe so much in my vowes, as to be at peace with all men, and make submissive amends where I have most displeased. Not basely feare-blasted or constraintively overruled, but purely pacifycatorie suppliant, for reconciliation and pardon doe I sue to the principallest of them, gainst whom I profest utter enmity. Even of Maister Doctor *Harvey,* I hartily desire the like, whose fame and reputation (though through some precedent injurious provocations, and fervent incitements of young heads) I rashly assailed: yet now better advised, and of his perfections more confirmedly perswaded, unfainedly I entreate of the whole worlde, from my penne his worths may receive no impeachment. All acknowledgements of aboundant Schollership, courteous well governed behaviour, and ripe experienst judgement, doe I attribute unto him. Onely with his milde gentle moderation, heerunto hath he wonne me.

Take my invective against him in that abject nature that you would doe the rayling of a Sophister in the schooles, or a scolding

Lawyer at the barre, which none but fooles wil wrest to defame. As the Tytle of this Booke is *Christs Teares,* so be this Epistle the Teares of my penne. Many things have I vainly sette forth whereof now it repenteth me. S. *Augustine* writ a whole booke of his Retractations. Nothing so much do I retract as that wherin soever I have scandaliz'd the meanest. Into some spleanative vaines of wantonnesse heeretofore have I foolishlie relapsed, to supply my private wants: of them no lesse doe I desire to be absolved then the rest, and to God & man doe I promise an unfained conversion.

Two or three triviall Volumes of mine, at this instant, are under the Printers hands, ready to be published, which being long bungled up before this, I must crave to be included in the Catalogue of mine excuse. To a little more witte have my encreasing yeeres reclaimed mee then I had before. Those that have beene perverted by any of my workes, let them reade this, and it shall thrice more benefite them. The Autumne I imitate, in sheading my leaves with the Trees, and so doth the Peacocke shead hys tayle. Buy who list, contemne who list, I leave every Reader his free libertie. If the best sort of men I content, I am satis-fiedly succes-full. Farewell all those that wish me wel, others wish I more wit to.

Tho. Nashe.

William Shakespeare, *Venus and Adonis*, 1593.

TO THE RIGHT HONORABLE

Henrie Wriothesley, Earle of Southampton

and Baron of Tichfield.

R*IGHT Honourable, I know not how I shall offend in dedicating my unpolisht lines to your Lordship, nor how the worlde will censure mee for choosing so strong a proppe to support so weake a burthen, onelye if your Honour seeme but pleased, I account my selfe highly praised, and vowe to take advantage of all idle houres, till I have honoured you with some graver labour. But if the first heire of my invention prove deformed, I shall be sorie it had so noble a god-father: and never after eare so barren a land, for feare it yeeld me still so bad a harvest, I leave it to your Honourable survey, and your Honor to your hearts content, which I wish may alwaies answere your owne wish and the worlds hopefull expectation.*

Your Honors in all dutie,
William Shakespeare.

Thomas Churchyard, *A Pleasant Conceite,* 1593–94.

To the Queenes most excellent *Majestie.*

MAY it please your Majestie, so long as breath is in my breast, life in the hart, and spirit in the heade, I cannot hold the hand from penning of some acceptable device to your Majestie, not to compare (in mine own over weening) with the rare Poets of our florishing age, but rather counterfeyting to sette foorth the workes of an extraordinarie Painter, that hath drawne in a pleasant conceite, divers flowers, fruites, and famous Townes: which pleasant conceite I have presumed (this Newe-yeeres day) to present to your Majestie, in signe and token that your gracious goodnesse towardes me oftentimes (and cheefely now for my pencyon) shal never goe out of my remembrance, with all dutifull services, belonging to a loyall subject. So under your princely favour & protection, praying for your prosperous preservation and Royall estate, I proceede to my purposed matter.

Your Majesties humble
Servaunt,
Thomas Churchyard.

Thomas Kyd, *Cornelia,* 1594.

To the vertuously Noble, and rightly honoured Lady, the *Countesse of Sussex.*

H*AVING no leysure (most noble Lady) but such as evermore is traveld with the afflictions of the minde, then which the world affoords no greater misery, it may bee wondred at by some how I durst undertake a matter of this moment, which both requireth cunning, rest and oportunity; but chiefely, that I would attempt the dedication of so rough, unpollished a worke to the survey of your so worthy selfe.*

But beeing well instructed in your noble and heroick dispositions, and perfectly assur'd of your honourable favours past (though neyther making needles glozes of the one, nor spoyling paper with the others Pharisaical embroderie), I have presum'd upon your true conceit and entertainement of these small endevours, that thus I purposed to make known my memory of you and them to be immortall.

A fitter present for a Patronesse so well accomplished I could not finde then this faire president of honour, magnanimitie, and love. Wherein, what grace that excellent Garnier *hath lost by my defaulte, I shall beseech your Honour to repaire with the regarde of those so bitter times and privie broken passions that I endured in the writing it.*

And so vouchsafing but the passing of a Winters weeke with desolate Cornelia, *I will assure your Ladiship my next Sommers better travell with the Tragedy of* Portia. *And ever spend one howre of the day in some kind service to your Honour, and another of the night in wishing you all happines. Perpetually thus devoting my poore selfe*

Your Honors in
all humblenes.
T. K.

William Percy, *Cœlia*, 1594.

TO THE READER.

COURTEOUS *Reader, whereas I was fullie determined to have concealed my Sonnets as thinges privie to my selfe, yet of courtesie having lent them to some, they were secretlie committed to the Presse and almost finished before it came to my knowledge. Wherefore making as they say,* Vertue of necessitie, *I did deeme it most convenient to præpose mine Epistle, onely to beseech you to account of them as of toyes and amorous devises; and ere long, I will impart unto the world another Poeme which shall be both more fruitfull and ponderous. In the meane while, I commit these as a pledge unto your indifferent censures. London,*

1594.

W. Percy.

William Shakespeare, *The Rape of Lucrece,* 1594.

TO THE RIGHT
HONOURABLE HENRY
Wriothesly, Earle of Southampton,
and Baron of Tichfield.

THE love I dedicate to your Lordship is without end: wherof this Pamphlet without beginning is but a superfluous Moity. The warrant I have of your Honourable disposition, not the worth of my untutord Lines makes it assured of acceptance. What I have done is yours, what I have to doe is yours, being part in all I have, devoted yours. Were my worth greater, my duety would shew greater, meane time, as it is, it is bound to your Lordship, to whom I wish long life still lengthned with all happinesse.

Your Lordships in all duety,
WILLIAM SHAKESPEARE.

Richard Barnfield, *Cynthia*, 1595.

To the Right Honourable, and most noble-minded Lorde, William Stanley, Earle of Darby, &c.

RIGHT Honorable, the dutifull affection I beare to your manie vertues, is cause, that to manifest my love to your Lordship, I am constrained to shew my simplenes to the world. Many are they that admire your worth, of the which number, I (though the meanest in abilitie, yet with the foremost in affection) am one that most desire to serve your Honour.

Small is the gift, but great is my good-will; the which, by how much the lesse I am able to expresse it, by so much the more it is infinite. Live long; and inherit your Predecessors vertues, as you do their dignitie and estate. This is my wish: the which your honorable excellent giftes doe promise me to obtaine: and whereof these few rude and unpollished lines, are a true (though and undeserving) testimony. If my ability were better, the signes should be greater; but being as it is, your honour must take me as I am, not as I should be. My yeares being so young, my perfection cannot be great. But howsoever it is, yours it is; and I my selfe am yours; in all humble service, most ready to be commaunded.

Richard Barnefeilde.

Richard Barnfield, *Cynthia,* 1595.

To the curteous Gentlemen Readers.

GENTLEMEN; *the last Terme there came forth a little toy of mine, intituled, The affectionate* Shepheard: *in the which, his Country* Content *found such friendly favor, that it hath incouraged me to publish my second fruites.* The affectionate Shepheard *being the first: howsoever undeservedly (I protest) I have beene thought (of some) to have beene the authour of two Books heretofore. I neede not to name them, because they are too-well knowne already: nor will I deny them, because they are dislik't; but because they are not mine. This protestation (I hope) will satisfie the indifferent: and as for them that are maliciously envious, as I cannot, so I care not to please. Some there were, that did interpret* The affectionate Shepheard, *otherwise then (in truth) I meant, touching the subject therof, to wit, the love of a Shepheard to a boy; a fault, the which I will not excuse, because I never made. Onely this, I will unshaddow my conceit: being nothing else, but an imitation of* Virgill, *in the second Eglogue of* Alexis. *In one or two places (in this Booke) I use the name of* Eliza *pastorally: wherein, lest any one should misconster my meaning (as I hope none will) I have briefly discovered my harmeles conceipt as concerning that name: whereof once (in a simple Shepheards device) I wrot this Epigramme.*

One name there is, which name above all other
I most esteeme, as time and place shall prove:

The one is *Vesta,* th' other *Cupids* Mother
The first my Goddesse is, the last my love;
Subject to Both I am: to that by berth;
To this for beautie; fairest on the earth.

Thus, hoping you will beare with my rude conceit of Cynthia, *(if for no other cause, yet, for that it is the first imitation of the verse of that excellent Poet, Maister* Spenser, *in his* Fayrie Queene) *I will leave you to the reading of that, which I so much desire may breed your Delight.*

Richard Barnefeild.

Francis Sabbie, *Pan's Pipe,* 1595.

To all youthfull Gentlemen,

Apprentises, favourers of the divine Arte of

sense-delighting Poesie.

GENTLEMEN, expect not in this my slender volume, amorous passions of some Courtly Lover, graced (as the custom is) with super fine rethoricall phrases. Look not here for some melodious ditties, descended from the wel-tuned strings of *Apollos* sweet-sounding Cittern. Here plainly have I presented unto your view rusticke *Tyterus,* rehearsing in rude countrey tearmes to his fellow *Thirsis* his happy blisse, and luckie fortune in obtayning the love of his desired *Phillida,* or clownish *Coridon,* one while taking and giving quaint taunts and privy quips of and to his froliking Copemates; one while againe contending for superiority, in tuning rurall ditties on *Pans* pastorall pipe. Now Gentlemen, if with *Coridon,* you shall find me not to play so well as the rest of my fellowes, my sole and humble request is, that you would not foorthwith proceed in condigne judgement against me, but with wise *Faustus* conceale your opinion, which doing, you shall animate, other wise altogether discourage a yong beginner.

Yours ever in curtesie.

F. S.

Sir Philip Sidney, *An Apologie for Poetry*, 1595.

To the Reader.

THE stormie Winter (deere Chyldren of the Muses) which hath so long held backe the glorious Sun-shine of divine Poesie, is heere by the sacred pen-breathing words of divine Sir *Phillip Sidney* not onely chased from our fame-inviting Clyme, but utterly for ever banisht eternitie. Then graciously regreet the perpetuall spring of ever-growing invention, and like kinde Babes, either enabled by wit or power, help to support me poore Midwife, whose daring adventure hath delivered from Oblivions wombe this ever-to-be-admired wits miracle. Those great ones who in themselves have interr'd this blessed innocent wil with *Aesculapius* condemne me as a detractor from their Deities: those who Prophet-like have but heard presage of his comming wil (if they wil doe wel) not onely defend, but praise mee, as the first publique bewrayer of Poesies *Messias*. Those who neither have seene, thereby to interre, nor heard, by which they might be inflamed with desire to see, let them (of duty) plead to be my Champions, sith both theyr sight and hearing by mine incurring blame is seasoned. Excellent Poesie (so created by this Apologie) be thou my Defendresse; and if any wound mee, let thy beautie (my soules Adamant) recure mee; if anie commend mine endevored hardiment, to them commend thy most divinest fury as a winged incouragement; so shalt thou have devoted to thee, and to them obliged,

Henry Olney.

Robert Southwell, *St. Peter's Complaint*, 1595.

THE AUTHOR TO HIS
loving Cosin.

P*OETS, by abusing their talent, & making the follies and faynings of love the customarie subject of their base endevours, have so discredited this facultie, that a Poet, a lover, and a lyar are by many reckoned but three words of one signification. But the vanitie of men cannot counterpoyse the authority of God, who delivering many parts of scripture in verse, and by his Apostle willing us to exercise our devotion in Hymnes & spirituall Sonnets, warranteth the Arte to be good, and the use allowable. And therfore not onely among the Heathen, whose Gods were chiefelie canonized by their Poets, and their Paynim Divinitie Oracled in verse; but even in the old & New Testament, it hath beene used by men of greatest Pietie, in matters of most devotion. Christ himselfe, by making a Hymne the conclusion of his last Supper, and the Prologue to the first Pageant of his Passion, gave his Spouse a methode to immitate, as in the office of the Church it appeareth; and to all men a patterne, to know the true use of this measured and footed stile. But the devill, as he affecteth Deitie and seeketh to have all the complements of Divine honour applied to his service, so hath hee among the rest possessed also most Poets with his idle fansies. For in lieu of solemne and devout matter, to which in dutie they owe their abilities, they now* *busie themselves in expressing such Passions as onely serve for testimonies to how unworthy affections they have wedded their wils. And because the best course to let them see the errour of their workes is to weave a new webbe in their owne loome, I have heere laid a few course threads together to invite some skilfuller wits to goe forward in the same or to begin some finer peece wherein it may be seene how well verse and vertue sute together. Blame me not (good Cosen) though I send you a blame-worthy present in which the most that can commende it is the good will of the writer, neither Arte nor invention giving it any credite. If in me this be a fault, you cannot be faultlesse that did importune mee to commit it, and therefore you must beare part of the pennance when it shall please sharpe censurers to impose it. In the meane time, with many good wishes I send you these few ditties. Add you the tunes, and let the Meane, I pray you, be still a part in all your Musick.*

Thomas Lodge, *A Margarite of America,* 1596.

To the noble, learned and vertuous Ladie, the Ladie *Russell, T. L.* wisheth affluence on earth, and felicitie in heaven.

M*ADAM, your deep and considerate judgement, your admired honor, & happy readings have drawne me to present this labor of mine to your gracious hands and favorable patronage: wherein, though you shall find nothing to admire, yet doubt I not but you may meet many things that deserve cherishing. Touching the subject, though of it selfe it seeme historicall, yet if it please you like our English* Sapho, *to look into that which I have slenderly written, I doubt not but that your memory shal acquaint you with my diligence, and my diligence may deserve your applause. Touching the place where I wrote this, it was in those straits christned by* Magelan; *in which place to the southward many wonderous Isles, many strange fishes, many monstrous Patagones withdrew my senses; briefly, many bitter and extreme frosts at midsummer continually clothe and clad the discomfortable mountaines; so that as there was great wonder in the place wherein I writ this, so likewise might it be marvelled, that in such scantie fare, such causes of feare, so mightie discouragements, and many crosses, I should deserve or eternize any thing. Yet what I have done (good Madame) judge* *and hope this felicitie from my pen, that whilst the memorie thereof shal live in any age, your charitie, learning, nobilitie and vertues shall be eternized.* Oppian *writing to* Theodosius *was as famous by the person to whome hee consecrated his study as fortunate in his labours, which, as yet, are not mastered by oblivion; so hope I (Madame) on the wing of your sacred name to be borne to the temple of Eternitie, where though envie barke at me, the Muses shall cherish, love, and happie me. Thus hoping your Ladiship will supply my boldnesse with your bountie and affabilitie, I humbly kisse your most delicate handes, shutting up my English duety under an Italian copie of humanitie and curtesie. From my house this 4. of Maie 1596.*

Your Honors in all zeale,

T. Lodge.

Thomas Lodge, *A Margarite of America*, 1596.

¶ *To the Gentlemen Readers.*

GENTLEMEN, I am prevented in mine own hopes; in seconding thrifts forward desires. Som foure yeres since being at sea with *M. Candish* (whose memorie if I repent not, I lament not) it was my chance in the librarie of the Jesuits in *Sanctum* to find this historie in the Spanish tong, which as I read delighted me, and delighting me, wonne me, and winning me, made me write it. The place where I began my worke, was a ship, where many souldiers of good reckning finding disturbed stomackes; it can not but stand with your discretions to pardon an undiscreete and unstaied penne, for hands may vary where stomacks miscary. The time I wrote in, was when I had rather will to get my dinner, then to win my fame. The order I wrote in was past order, where I rather observed mens hands lest they should strike me, then curious reason of men to condemne mee. In a worde, I wrote under hope rather the fish should eate both me writing and my paper written then fame should know me, hope should acquaint her with me, or any but miserie should heare mine ending. For those faults (gentlemen) escaped by the Printer, in not being acquainted with my hand, and the booke printed in my absence, I must crave you with favour to judge of, and with your wonted curtesies to correct; and according to Ecclesiasticall law, give us on our confesion absolution. If you will not, remember this, that a countrie lasse for Ladies, may tell them they curle too much; and for Gentlemen, that they are unfashioned by their fashions. To be short, who lives in this world, let him wincke in the world; for either men proove too blinde in seeing too litle, or too presumptuous in condemning that they shoulde not.

Yours T. Lodge.

Edmund Spenser, *The Faerie Queene,* 1596.

TO
THE MOST HIGH,
MIGHTIE
And
MAGNIFICENT
EMPRESSE RENOW-
MED FOR PIETIE, VER-
TUE, AND ALL GRATIOUS
GOVERNMENT ELIZABETH BY
THE GRACE OF GOD QUEENE
OF ENGLAND FRANCE AND
IRELAND AND OF VIRGI-
NIA, DEFENDOUR OF THE
FAITH, &c. HER MOST
HUMBLE SERVANT
EDMUND SPENSER
DOTH IN ALL HU-
MILITIE DEDI-
CATE, PRE-
SENT
AND CONSECRATE THESE
HIS LABOURS TO LIVE
WITH THE ETERNI-
TIE OF HER
FAME.

Francis Bacon, *Essayes,* 1597.

To M. Anthony Bacon
his deare Brother.

LOVING and beloved Brother, I do nowe like some that have an Orcharde ill neighbored, that gather their fruit before it is ripe, to prevent stealing. These fragments of my conceites were going to print. To labour the staie of them had bin troublesome, and subject to interpretation; to let them passe had beene to adventure the wrong they mought receive by untrue Coppies, or by some garnishment, which it mought please any that shold set them forth to bestow upon them. Therefore I helde it best discreation to publish them my selfe as they passed long agoe from my pen, without any further disgrace, then the weakenesse of the Author. And as, I did ever hold, there mought be as great a vanitie in retiring and withdrawings mens conceites (except they bee of some nature) from the world, as in obtruding them; so in these particulars I have played my selfe the Inquisitor, and find nothing to my understanding in them contrarie, or infectious to the state of Religion, or manners, but rather (as I suppose) medicinable. Only I disliked now to put them out because they will bee like the late newe halfe-pence, which though the Silver were good, yet the peeces were small. But since they would not stay with their Master, but would needes travaile abroade, I have preferred them to you, that are next myselfe, Dedicating them, such as they are, to our love, in the depth whereof (I assure you) I sometimes wish your infirmities translated upon my selfe, that her Majestie mought have the service of so active and able a mind, & I mought be with excuse confined to these contemplations & studies for which I am fittest, so commende I you to the preservation of the divine Majestie. From my Chamber at Graies Inne, this 30. of Januarie, 1597.

Your entire Loving brother.
Fran. Bacon.

Nicholas Breton, *The Scholler and the Souldiour,* 1597.

To the Courteous and gentle Reader.

GENTLE Reader, reade no further then you like. If you finde any thing to your Content, thinke well of mee for my paines. If there be nothing that likes you, my lucke is nought. In nothing there can be no great thing, yet something may bee founde, though nothing to any great purpose. Well, there are divers Nothings which you shall reade further off if you will take paines to turne over the leafe and peruse the rest that followes. Now, though I will wish you looke for no mervailous or worthy thing, yet shall you finde something, though in effect (as it were) nothing, yet in conceit a pretie thing to passe away the time withal. Wel, if you stande content with this Nothing, it may bee ere long, I will send you something, more to your liking: till when, I wish you nothing but well. And so I bid you farewell, from my Chamber at the blacke Friers.

N. B.

John Dowland, *The First Book of Songs or Airs*, 1597.

TO THE RIGHT HONOURABLE SIR GEORGE CAREY, OF THE MOST HONORABLE ORDER OF THE GARTER KNIGHT:

Baron of Hunsdon, Captaine of her Majesties gentlemen Pensioners,

Governor of the Isle of Wight, Lieutenant of the countie of South.

Lord Chamberlaine of her Majesties most Royall house, and of

her Highnes most honourable Privie Counsell.

THAT *harmony (Right Honorable) which is skilfullie exprest by Instruments, albeit, by reason of the variety of number & proportion of it selfe, it easilie stirs up the minds of the hearers to admiration & delight, yet for higher authoritie and power, hath been ever worthily attributed to that kinde of Musicke which to the sweetnes of instrument applies the lively voice of man, expressing some worthy sentence or excellent Poeme. Hence (as al antiquitie can witnesse) first grew the heavenly Art of musicke: for* Linus, Orpheus, *and the rest, according to the number and time of their Poemes, first framed the numbers and times of musicke. So that* Plato *defines melody to consist of harmony, number, & wordes: harmony, naked of it selfe; words, the ornament of harmony; number, the common friend & writer of them both. This small booke containing the consent of speaking harmony, joyned with the most musicall in-*

strument, the Lute, being my first labour, I have presumed to dedicate to your Lordship: who, for your vertue & nobility, are best able to protect it; and for your honourable favors towards me, best deserving my duety and service. Besides, your noble inclination and love to all good Artes, and namely the divine science of musicke, doth challenge the patronage of all learning; then which no greater title can bee added to Nobilitie. Neither in these your honours, may I let passe the dutifull remembrance of your vertuous Lady, my honourable mistris, whose singular graces towards me have added spirit to my unfortunate labours. What time and diligence I have bestowed in the search of Musicke, what travel in forren countries, what successe and estimation, even among strangers, I have found, I leave to the report of others. Yet all this in vaine, were it not that your honorable hands have vouchsaft to uphold my poore fortunes: which I now wholy recommend to your gratious protection, with these my first endevors, humbly beseeching you to accept and cherish them with your continued favours.

Your Lordships most humble servant,
John Dowland.

John Dowland, *The First Book of Songs or Airs*, 1597.

To the courteous Reader.

HOW hard an enterprise it is, in this skilfull and curious age, to commit our private labours to the publike view, mine owne disabilitie and others hard successe doe too well assure me: and were it not for that love I beare to the true lovers of musicke, I had concealde these my first fruits; which how they will thrive with your taste I know not, howsoever the greater part of them might have been ripe inough by their age. The Courtly judgement, I hope, will not be severe against them, being it selfe a party; and those sweet springs of humanity (I meane our two famous Universities) wil entertain them for his sake whome they have already grac't, and, as it were, enfranchisd in the ingenuous profession of Musicke: which, from my childhoode, I have ever aymed at, sundry times leaving my native countrey, the better to attain so excellent a science. About sixteene yeeres past, I travelled the chiefest parts of France, a nation furnisht with great variety of Musicke; but lately, being of a more confirmed judgement, I bent my course toward the famous provinces of Germany, where I founde both excellent masters, and most honorable Patrons of Musicke, namely, those two miracles of this age for vertue and magnificence, *Henry Julio,* Duke of *Brunswick,* and learned *Maritius, Lantzgrave* of *Hessen;* of whose princely vertues and favors towards me I can never speake sufficientlie. Neither can I forget the kindnes of *Alexandro Horologio,* a right learned master of Musicke, servant to the royal Prince, the *Lantzgrave* of *Hessen,* and *Gregorio Howet,* Lutenist to the magnificent Duke of *Brunswick;* both whome I name, as well for their love to me as also for their excellency in their faculties. Thus having spent some moneths in *Germany,* to my great admiration of that worthy country; I past over the Alpes into *Italy,* where I founde the Cities furnisht with all good Artes, but especiallie Musicke. What favour and estimation I had in *Venice, Padua, Genoa, Ferrara, Florence,* & divers other places, I willingly suppresse, least I should, any way seeme partiall in mine owne indevours. Yet can I not dissemble the great content I found in the proferd amity of the most famous *Luca Marenzio,* whose sundry letters I received from Rome; and one of them, because it is but short, I have thought good to set downe, not thinking it any disgrace to be proud of the judgement of so excellent a man.

Molto Magnifico Signior mio osservandissimo.

PER una lettera del Signior Alberigo Malvezi ho inteso quanto con cortese affetto si mostri desideroso di essermi congionto d'amicitia, dove infinitamente la ringratio di questo suo buon' animo, offerendomegli all'incontro se in alcuna cosa la posso servire, poi che gli meriti delle sue infinite virtù, e qualità meritano che ogni uno e me l'ammirino e osservino, e per fine di questo le bascio le mani. Di Roma, a' 13. di Luglio. 1595.

D.V.S. Affettionatissimo servitore,

Luca Marenzio.

John Dowland, *The First Book of Songs or Airs,* 1597.

NOT to stand to long upon my travels, I will onely name that worthy maister, *Giovanni Crochio,* Vice master of the chappel of S. Marks in *Venice;* with whome I had familiar conference. And thus what experience I could gather abroad, I am now ready to practise at home, if I may but find encouragement in my first assaies. There have bin divers Lute lessons of mine lately printed without my knowledge, falce and unperfect; but I purpose shortly my selfe to set forth the choisest of all my Lessons in print, and also an Introduction for fingering; with other books of Songs, whereof this is the first. And as this findes favour with you, so shal I be affected to labor in the rest. *Farewell.*

John Dowland.

Thomas Middleton, *The Wisdom of Solomon Paraphrased,* 1597.

To the right Honourable and my *very good Lord, Robert Devoreux, Erle* of Essex and Ewe, Vicount of Hereford, Lorde Ferrers of Chartley, Bourcher, and Louayne, Maister *of her Majesties Horse and Ordonance, Knight of the ho-* nourable order of the Garter, and one of her Majesties most honorable privie Counsell.

THE Summers Harvest (right Honourable) is long since reapt, & now it is sowing time againe. Behold, I have scattred a few seedes upon the yong ground of unskilfulnesse. If it beare fruit, my labour is well bestowed; but if it be barren, I shall have lesse joy to set more. The husbandman observes the courses of the Moone, I, the forces of your favor: he desireth sun-shine, I, cheerefull countenance: which once obtayned, my harvest of joy will soone bee ripened. My seedes, as yet, lodge in the bosome of the earth, like Infantes upon the lappe of a Favourite, wanting the budding spring-time of their growth, not knowing the Est of their glorie, the west of their quietnesse, the South of their summer, the North of their winter; but if the beames of your aspectes lighten the small moytie of a smaller implanting, I shall have an every-day-harvest, a fruition of content, a braunch of felicitie.

Your Honours addicted in all observance,
Thomas Midleton.

Thomas Middleton, *The Wisdom of Solomon Paraphrased*, 1597.

To the Gentlemen-Readers.

G*ENTLEMEN, I give you the surveyaunce of my new-bought grounde, and will only stand unto your verdicts. I feare me, that the acres of my fields passe the anchers of my seed, if wanting seed, then I hope it wil not be to much seeded. This is my bare excuse: but trust me, had my wit been sufficient to maintaine the freedome of my will, then both should have been answerable to your wishes, yet neverthelesse thinke of it as a willing, though not a fulfilling moity. But what meane I? While I thus argue,* Momus *and* Zoylus, *those two Ravens devoure my feede, because I lacke a Scarrecrowe: indeede so I may have lesse than I have, when such fowle-gutted Ravens swallowe up my portion. If you gape for stuffing, hie you to dead carrion carkasses, and make them your Ordinaries. I beseeche you Gentlemen, let mee have your ayde, and as you have seene the first practise of my husbandry in sowing, so let me have your helping hands unto my reaping.*

Yours devoted in friendship.
Thomas Middleton

Thomas Deloney, *The Gentle Craft,*
The Second Part, 1598.

To the Courteous Readers
health

GENTLE Reader, you that vouchsafe to cast curteous lookes into this rude Pamphlet, expect not herein to find any matter of light value, curiously pen'd with pickt words, or choise phrases, but a quaint and plaine discourse best fitting matters of merriment, seeing wee have herein no cause to talke of Courtiers or Scholers. Notwithstanding, if you find your selfe over-charged with melancholy, you may perhaps have here a fit medicien to purge that humour, by conferring in this place with Doctor *Burket:* or if you meet with round *Robin,* he may chance ryme it away. I tell you among Shoomakers in some solace, as you shall see by *Tom Drums* entertainment, and other mad merry prankes playd by the Greene-King of S. Martins. If that will not suffice, you may, in meeting with *Anthony now now,* have such a fit of mirth, with his firking Fiddle, that it shall be a great cause to expell choler. And so I leave you to your owne liking, whether you will enter to see this sport or no: stand backe, I pray, roome for a Gentleman, for you cannot come in under a groat.

Christopher Marlowe and George Chapman,
Hero and Leander, 1598.

To the Right Worshipfull, Sir Thomas Walsingham, Knight.

SIR, *we thinke not our selves discharged of the duty we owe to our friend when we have brought the breathles bodie to the earth; for albeit the eye there taketh his ever farewell of that beloved object, yet the impression of the man that hath been deare unto us, living an after life in our memorie, there putteth us in minde of farther obsequies due unto the deceased; and namely of the performance of whatsoever we may judge shall make to his living credit and to the effecting of his determinations prevented by the stroke of death. By these meditations (as by an intellectuall will) I suppose my selfe executor to the unhappily deceased author of this Poem; upon whom knowing that in his life time you bestowed many kinde favours, entertaining the parts of reckoning and worth which you found in him with good countenance and liberall affection, I cannot but see so far into the will of him dead, that whatsoever issue of his braine should chance to come abroad, that the first breath it should take might be the gentle aire of your liking; for, since his selfe had been accustomed therunto, it would prove more agreeable and thriving to his right children than any other foster countenance whatsoever. At this time seeing that this unfinished Tragedy happens under my hands to be imprinted; of a double duty, the one to your selfe, the other to the deceased, I present the same to your most favourable allowance, offering my utmost selfe now and ever to be readie,*

at your Worships

disposing:

E. B.

John Marston, *The Scourge of Villainy*, 1598.

To his most esteemed and best beloved Self dat dedicat que.

To those that seeme judiciall perusers.

KNOW, I hate to affect too much obscuritie & harshnes because they profit no sence. To note vices, so that no man can understand them, is as fonde as the French execution in picture. Yet there are some (too many) that think nothing good that is so curteous as to come within their reach. Tearming all Satyres bastard which are not palpable darke, and so rough writ that the hearing of them read would set a man's teeth on edge. For whose unseasond pallate I wrote the first Satyre, in some places too obscure, in all places misliking me. Yet when by some scurvie chaunce it shal come into the late perfumed fist of judiciall *Torquatus* (that, like some rotten stick in a troubled water, hath gotte a great deale of barmy froth to stick to his sides) I know he will vouchsafe it, some of his new-minted Epithets (as *Reall, Intrinsecate, Delphicke*), when in my conscience hee understands not the least part of it. But from thence proceedes his judgement. *Perseus* is crabby, because ancient, and his jerkes (being perticulerly given to private customes of his time) duskie. *Juvenall* (upon the like occasion) seemes to our judgement gloomie. Yet both of them goe a good seemely pace, not stumbling, shuffling. *Chaucer* is harde even to our understandings: who knowes not the reason? Howe much more those old Satyres which expresse themselves in termes that breathed not long even in their daies. But had we then lived, the understanding of them had been nothing hard. I will not deny there is a seemely decorum to be observed, and a peculiar kinde of speech for a Satyre's lips, which I can willinglier conceive then dare to prescribe; yet let me have the substance rough, not the shadow. I cannot, nay, I will not delude your sight with mists; yet I dare defend my plainnes gainst the verjuyce face of the crabbed'st Satyrist that ever stuttered. Hee that thinks worse of my rimes then my selfe, I scorne him, for he cannot; he that thinks better is a foole. So favour mee, *Good-Opinion,* as I am farre from beeing a *Suffenus.* If thou perusest mee with an unpartiall eye, reade on: if otherwise, knowe I neyther value thee, nor thy censure. *W. Kinsayder.*

John Bodenham, *Belvedere*, 1600.

To the Reader.

IT shall be needlesse (gentle Reader) to make any Apologie for the defence of this labour because the same being collected from so many singular mens workes and the worth of them all having been so especially approoved and past with no meane applause the censure of all in generall doth both disburden me of that paines and sets the better approbation on this excellent booke. It shall be sufficient for me then to tell thee, that here thou art brought into the Muses Garden, (a place that may beseeme the presence of the greatest Prince in the world.) Imagine then thy height of happinesse, in being admitted to so celestiall a Paradise. Let thy behaviour then (while thou art here) answere thy great fortune, and make use of thy time as so rich a treasure requireth.

The walkes, alleys, and passages in this Garden are almost infinite; every where a turning, on all sides such windings in and out: yet all extending both to pleasure and profit, as very rare or seldome shalt thou see the like. Marke then, what varietie of flowres grow all along as thou goest, and trample on none rudely, for all are right precious. If thy conscience be wounded, here are store of hearbs to heale it. If thy doubts be fearefull, here are flowres of comfort. Are thy hopes frustrated? Here's immediate helpes for them. In briefe, what infirmitie canst thou have, but here it may bee cured? What delight or pleasure wouldst thou have, but here it is affoorded?

Concerning the nature and qualitie of these excellent flowres, thou seest that they are most learned, grave, and wittie sentences; each line being a severall sentence, and none exceeding two lines at the uttermost. All which, being subjected under apt and proper heads, as arguments what is then dilated and spoken of: even so each head that first his definition in a couplet sentence; then the single and double sentences by variation of letter do follow: and lastly, Similies and Examples in the same nature likewise, to conclude every Head or Argument handled. So let this serve to shew thee the whole intent of this worke.

Now that every one may be fully satisfied concerning this Garden, that no one man doth assume to him-selfe the praise thereof, or can arrogate to his owne deserving those things which have been derived from so many rare and ingenious spirits, I have set down both how, whence, and where these flowres had their first springing, till thus they were drawne togither into the *Muses Garden,* that every ground may challenge his owne, each plant his particular, and no one be injuried in the justice of his merit.

First, out of many excellent speeches spoken to her Majestie, at Tiltings, Triumphes, Maskes, Shewes, and devises perfourmed in prograce: as also out of divers choise Ditties sung to her; and some especially, proceeding from her owne most sacred selfe: Here are great store of them digested into their meete places, according as the method of the worke plainly delivereth. Likewise out of privat Poems, Sonnets, Ditties, and other wittie conceits, given to her Honorable Ladies and vertuous Maids of Honour; according as they could be obtained by sight, or favour of coppying, a number of most wittie and singular Sentences.

Secondly, looke what workes of Poetrie have been put to the worlds eye, by that learned and right royall king and Poet, James king of Scotland, no one Sentence of worth hath escaped, but are likewise here reduced into their right roome and place.

Next, out of sundry things extant, and many in privat, done by these right Honourable persons following: *Thomas, Earle of Surrey, The Lord Marquesse of Winchester, Mary, Countesse of Pembrooke, Sir Philip Sidney.*

From Poems and workes of these noble personages, extant: *Edward, Earle of Oxenford, Ferdinando, Earle of Derby, Sir Walter Raleigh, Sir Edward Dyer, Fulke Grevile, Esquier, Sir John Harrington.*

From divers essayes of their Poetrie; some extant among other Honourable personages writings; some from private labours and translations: *Edmund Spencer, Henry Constable Esquier, Samuell Daniell, Thomas Lodge, Doctor of Physicke, Thomas Watson, Michaell Drayton, John Davies, Thomas Hudson, Henrie Locke Esquier, John Marstone, Christopher Marlow, Benjamin Johnson, William Shakspeare, Thomas Churchyard Esquier, Thomas Nash, Thomas Kidde, George Peele, Robert Greene, Jusuah Sylvester, Nicholas Breton, Gervase Markham, Thomas Storer, Robert Wilmot, Christopher Middleton, Richard Barnefield.*

These being Moderne and extant Poets, that have liv'd togither; from many of their extant workes, and some kept in privat: *Thomas Norton Esquier, George Gascoigne Esquier, Frauncis Kindlemarsh Esquier, Thomas Atchlow, George Whetstones.*

These being deceased, have left divers extant labours, and many more held back from publishing, which for the most part have been perused, and their due right here given them in the Muses Garden.

Besides, what excellent Sentences have been in any presented Tragedie, Historie, Pastorall, or Comedie, they have been likewise gathered, and are here inserted in their proper places.

John Bodenham, *England's Helicon,* 1600.

To his very loving friends, M. Nicholas *Wanton* and M. *George Faucet.*

T*HOUGH many miles (but more occasions) doo sunder us (kinde Gentlemen) yet a promise at parting dooth in justice claime performance, and assurance of gentle acceptance, would mightilie condemne me if I should neglect it.* Helicon, *though not as I could wish, yet in such good sort as time would permit, having past the pikes of the Presse, comes now to* Yorke *to salute her rightfull Patrone first, and next (as his deere friends and kindsmen) to offer you her kinde service. If shee speede well there, it is all shee requires; if they frowne at her heere, she greatly not cares: for the wise (shee knowes) will never be other then them selves: as for such then as would seeme so, but neither are, nor ever will be, she holds this as a maine principle; that their malice neede as little be feared, as their favour or friendship is to be desired. So hoping you will not forget us there, as we continuallie shall be mindefull of you heere, I leave you to the delight of* Englands Helicon.

Yours in all he may,
A. B.

John Bodenham, *England's Helicon*, 1600.

To the Reader, if indifferent.

MANY honoured names have heretofore (in their particuler interest) patronized some part of these inventions: many here be, that onely these Collections have brought to light, & not inferiour (in the best opinions) to anie before published. The travaile that hath beene taken in gathering them from so many handes, hath wearied some howres, which severed, might in part have perished, digested into this meane volume, may in the opinion of some not be altogether unworthy the labour. If any man hath beene defrauded of any thing by him composed, by another mans title put to the same, hee hath this benefit by this collection, freely to challenge his owne in publique, where els he might be robd of his proper due. No one thing beeing here placed by the Collector of the same under any mans name, eyther at large, or in letters, but as it was delivered by some especiall coppy comming to his handes. No one man, that shall take offence that his name is published to any invention of his, but he shall within the reading of a leafe or two, meete with another in reputation every way equal with himselfe, whose name hath beene before printed to his Poeme, which nowe taken away were more then theft: which may satisfie him that would faine seeme curious, or be intreated for his fame.

John Bodenham, *England's Helicon*, 1600.

NOWE, if any Stationer shall finde faulte, that his Coppies, are robd by any thing in this Collection, let me aske him this question: Why more in this, then in any Divine or humaine Authour? From whence a man (writing of that argument) shal gather any saying, sentence, similie, or example, his name put to it who is the Author of the same. This is the simplest of many reasons that I could urdge, though perhaps the neerest his capacitie, but that I would be loth to trouble my selfe to satisfie him. Further, if any man whatsoever, in prizing of his owne birth or fortune, shall take in scorne, that a far meaner man in the eye of the world shal be placed by him: I tell him plainly whatsoever so excepting that, that mans wit is set by his, not that man by him. In which degree, the names of Poets (all feare and dutie ascribed to her great and sacred Name) have beene placed with the names of the greatest Princes of the world, by the most autentique and worthiest judgements, without disparagement to their soveraigne titles: which if any man taking exception thereat, in ignorance know not, I hold him unworthy to be placed by the meanest that is but graced with the title of a Poet. Thus, gentle Reader, I wish thee all happines.

L. N.

Thomas Dekker, *The Shomakers Holiday*, 1600.

To all good Fellowes, Professors of *the Gentle Craft; of what degree* soever.

KINDE Gentlemen, and honest boone Companions, I present you here with a merrie conceited Comedie, called, *the Shoomakers Holyday,* acted by my Lorde Admiralls Players this present Christmasse, before the Queenes most excellent Majestie, for the mirth and pleasant matter, by her Highnesse graciously accepted; being indeede no way offensive. The Argument of the play I will set downe in this Epistle: Sir *Hugh Lacie* Earle of *Lincolne,* had a yong Gentleman of his owne name, his nere kinsman, that loved the Lorde Mayors daughter of London; to prevent and crosse which love, the Earle caused his kinsman to be sent Coronell of a companie into France: who resigned his place to another gentleman his friend, and came disguised like a Dutch Shoomaker, to the house of *Symon Eyre* in Tower streete, who served the Mayor and his houshold with shooes. The merriments that passed in Eyres house, his comming to be Mayor of *London, Lacies* getting his love, and other accidents; with two merry Three-mens songs. Take all in good worth that is well intended, for nothing is purposed but mirth, mirth lengthneth long life; which, with all other blessings I heartily wish you.

Farewell.

William Kemp, *Kemp's Nine Daies Wonder*, 1600.

To the true Ennobled Lady, and his most bountifull Mistris, Mistris *Anne Fitton,* Mayde of honour to the most sacred Mayde Royall Queene *Elizabeth.*

Honorable Mistris,

IN the waine of my little wit, I am forst to desire your protection, else every Ballad-singer will proclaime me bankrupt of honesty. A sort of mad fellows, seeing me merrily disposd in a Morrice, have so bepainted mee in print, since my gambols began from London to Norwich, that (having but an ill face before) I shall appeare to the world without a face, if your fayre hand wipe not away their foule coulors. One hath written *Kemps farewell,* to the tune of *Kery, mery, Buffe:* another, his desperate daungers in his late travaile: the third, his entertainement to New-Market, which towne I came never neere by the length of halfe the heath. Some sweare in a Trenchmore I have trode a good way to winne the world: others that guesse righter, affirme, I have without good help daunst myselfe out of the world. Many say many thinges that were never thought. But, in a word, your poore servant offers the truth of his progresse and profit to your honorable view. Receive it, I beseech you, such as it is, rude and plaine, for I know your pure judgement lookes as soone to see beauty in a Blackamoore, or heare smooth speech from a Stammerer, as to finde any thing, but blunt mirth in a Morrice dauncer, especially such a one as *Will Kemp,* that hath spent his life in mad Jigges and merry jestes. Three reasons moove mee to make publik this journey, one, to reprove lying fooles I never knew: the other, to commend loving friends, which, by the way, I daily found: the third, to shew my duety to your honorable selfe, whose favours (among other bountiful friends) makes me (dispight of this sad world) judge my hart Corke, & my heeles feathers, so that, me-thinkes, I could flye to Rome (at least, hop to Rome, as the olde Proverb is) with a morter on my head. In which light conceite, I lowly begge pardon and leave, for my Tabrer strikes his hunts up, I must to Norwich. Imagine, Noble Mistris, I am now setting from my Lord Mayors, the houre, about seaven; the morning, gloomy; the company, many; my hart, merry.

Your worthy Ladyships most,
unworthy servant,
William Kemp.

Nicholas Breton, *A True Description of Unthankfulnesse,* 1602.

To the Reader.

HEE that is unthankfull for a good turne, sheweth the venime of a vile Nature, and hee that is kindly gratefull, is worthie to bee beeloved. If you bee of the last condition, I commend you; if of the first, God amend you. What you are, I know not; but I hope the best, the worst I desire not to heare off. And therefore, in briefe, the Treatise beeing short, I will not trouble you to long, but as I finde your kindnesse, will rest in thankfulnesse.

Your friend
Nicholas Breton.

Thomas Campion, *Observations in the Art of English Poesy*, 1602.

To the Right Noble and worthily honourd, the Lord *Buckhurst, Lord High Treasurer of England.*

IN two things (right honorable) it is generally agreed that man excels all other creatures, in reason and speech: and in them by how much one man surpasseth an other, by so much the neerer he aspires to a celestiall essence.

Poesy in all kind of speaking is the chiefe beginner, and maintayner of eloquence, not only helping the eare with the acquaintance of sweet numbers, but also raysing the minde to a more high and lofty conceite. For this end have I studyed to induce a true forme of versefying into our language: for the vulgar and unarteficiall custome of riming hath, I know, deter'd many excellent wits from the exercise of English Poesy. The observations which I have gathered for this purpose I humbly present to your Lordship, as to the noblest judge of Poesy, and the most honorable protector of all industrious learning; which if your Honour shall vouchsafe to receive, who both in your publick and private Poemes have so devinely crowned your fame, what man will dare to repine or not strive to imitate them? Wherefore, with all humility I subject my selfe and them to your gratious favour, beseeching you in the noblenes of your mind to take in worth so simple a present, which by some worke drawne from my more serious studies, I will hereafter endevour to excuse.

Your Lordships humbly devoted,

THOMAS CAMPION.

Francis Davison, *Poeticall Rhapsody*, 1602.

To the Reader.

BEING induced, by some private reasons, and by the instant intreatie of speciall friendes, to suffer some of my worthlesse Poems to be published, I desired to make some written by my deere friend *Anomos,* and my deerer *Brother,* to beare them company, both without their consent, the latter being in the low Country Warres, and the former utterly ignorant thereof. My friendes name I concealed, mine owne, and my brothers, I willed the Printer to suppresse, as well as I had concealed the other, which he having put in, without my privity, we must both now undergoe a sharper censure perhaps then our nameles works should have done, & I especially. For if their Poems be liked, the praise is due to their invention, if disliked, the blame both by them, and all men will be derived uppon me, for publishing that which they meant to suppresse.

If thou thinke wee affect fame by these kindes of writings, though I thinke them no disparagement even to the best judgements, yet I answere in all our behalfes, with the Princely Shepheard *Dorus:*

Our hearts doe seeke another estimation.

If thou condemne Poetry in generall, and affirme, that it doth intoxicate the braine, and make men utterly unfit, either for more serious studies, or for any active course of life, I only say, *Jubeo te stultum esse libenter.* Since experience proves by examples of many, both dead and living, that divers delighted and excelling herein, being Princes or States-men, have governed and counceled as wisely, being Souldiers, have commanded armies as fortunately, being Lawyers, have pleaded as judicially and eloquently, being Divines, have written and taught as profoundly, and being of any other Profession, have discharged it as sufficiently as any other men whatsoever. If liking other kindes, thou mislike the Lyricall, because the chiefest subject thereof is Love; I reply, that Love being virtuously intended, & worthily placed, is the Whetstone of witt, and Spurre to all generous actions; and that many excellent spirits with great fame of witt, and no staine of judgement, have written excellently in this kind, and specially the ever-praise worthy *Sidney.* So as if thou will needs make it a fault, for mine owne part,

Haud timeo, si iam nequeo defendere crimen
Cum tanto commune viro.

If any except against the mixing (both at the beginning and ende of this booke) of diverse thinges written by great and learned Personages, with our meane and worthles Scriblings, I utterly disclaime it, as being done by the Printer, either to grace the forefront with Sir *Ph. Sidneys,* and others names, or to make the booke grow to a competent volume.

For these Poems in particular, I could aledge these excuses: that those under the Name of *Anomos,* were written (as appeareth by divers things to Syr *Philip Sidney* living, and of him dead) almost twentie yeers since, when Poetry was farre from that perfection to which it hath now attained; that my Brother is by profession a Souldier, and was not 18. yeeres old when hee writt these

Toyes; that mine owne were made most of them sixe or seven yeeres since, at idle times as I journeyed up and downe during my Travails. But to leave their workes to justifie themselves, or the Authors to justifie their workes, and to speake of myne owne: thy mislikes I contemne, thy prayses (which I neither deserve, nor expect), I esteeme not, as hoping (God willing) ere long, to regaine thy good Opinion, if lost, or more deservedly to continue it, if already obtained, by some graver Worke. *Farewell.*

FRA: DAVISON.

Sir William Alexander, *Aurora,* 1604.

TO THE RIGHT HONORABLE AND VERTUOUS Lady, the Lady Agnes Dowglas, *Countesse of Argyle.*

MADAME, when I remember the manie obligations which I owe to your manifold merits, I oftentimes accuse my selfe to my self of forgetfulnes, and yet I am to be excused: for how can I satisfie so infinit a debt, since whilst I go to disengage my self in some measure by giving you the patronage of these unpolished lines (which indeed for their manie errors, had need of a respected Sanctuary) I but engage my self further, while as you take the patronage of so unpolished lines. Yet this shal not discourage me, for alwayes I carie this advantage, that as they were the fruits of beautie, so shal they be sacrificed as oblations to beautie. And to a beautie, though of it selfe most happie, yet more happie in this, that it is thought worthie (and can be no more then worthy) to be the outward cover of so many inward perfections. So assuring my selfe, that as no darknesse can abide before the Sunne, so no deformitie can be found in those papers, over which your eyes have once shined. I rest

Your Honors most humbly
devoted,
William Alexander.

John Marston, *The Malcontent,* 1604.

To the Reader.

I AM an ill Oratur; and, in truth, use to indite more honestly then eloquently, for t'is my custome to speake as I think, and write as I speake.

In plainenesse, therefore, understand, that in some things I have willingly erred, as in supposing a Duke of *Genoa,* and in taking names different from that Citties families: for which some may wittily accuse me; but my defence shall bee as honest, as many reproofes unto mee have been most malicious. Since (I heartily protest) t'was my care to write so farre from reasonable offence, that even strangers, in whose State I layd my Scene, should not from thence draw any disgrace to any, dead or living. Yet in despight of my indevors, I understand, some have bin most unadvisedly over-cunning in mis-interpreting me, & with subtilty (as deep as hell) have maliciously spread ill rumours, which springing from themselves, might to themselves have heavily returned. Surely I desire to satisfie every firme spirit, who, in all his actions, proposeth to himself no more ends then God and vertue doe, whose intentions are alwayes simple. To such I protest, that with my free understanding, I have not glanced at disgrace of any, but of those, whose unquiet studies labor innovation, contempt of holy policie, reverent comely superiority, and established unity. For the rest of my supossed tartnesse, I feare not, but unto every worthy mind t'will be approoved so generall and honest, as may modestly passe with the freedome of a Satyre. I would faine leave the paper; onely one thing afflicts mee, to thinke that Scenes, invented, meerely to be spoken, should be inforcively published to be read, & that the least hurt I can receive, is to do my selfe the wrong. But, since others otherwise would doe me more, the least inconvenience is to be accepted. I have my selfe, therefore, set forth this Comedy; but so, that my inforced absence must much relye upon the Printers discretion: but I shall intreat, slight errors in orthography may bee as slightly or'e-passed; and that the unhandsome shape which this trifle in reading presents, may bee pardoned, for the pleasure it once afforded you, when it was presented with the soule of lively action.

Sine aliqua dementia nullus Phaebus.

J. M.

Antony Scoloker, *Daiphantus*, 1604.

TO THE MIGHTIE, LEARNED, and Ancient Potentate *Quisquis;* Emperour of ✠ King of Great and Little *A.* Prince of *B. C.* and *D.&c.*

Aliquis, wisheth the much increase of true Subjects, free from *Passion Spleene,* and *Melancholy:* and indued with Vertue, Wisedome, and Magnanimitie.

Or, to the Reader.

AN Epistle *to the* Reader; *why? That must have his Forehead, or first Entrance like a Courtier,* Faire-spoken, *and full of* Expectation; *his middle or Center like your Citizens ware-house, beautified with inticing vanities, though the true Riches consist of Bald Commodities; his Randevow or conclusion like the Lawyers Case, able to pocket up any matter. But let good word be your best* Evidence. *In the Generall or Foundation, he must be like* Paules-Church, *resolved to let every* Kinght *and* Gull *travell upon him, yet his Particulars or Lyneaments may be Royall as the* Exchange, *with ascending steps, promising Newe but costly devices & fashions. It must have Teeth like a* Satyre, *Eyes like a* Cryticke, *and yet may your Tongue speake false* Latine, *like your Panders and Bawdes of* Poetrie. *Your* Genius *and* Species *should march in battle aray with our Politicians; yet your* Genius *ought to live with an honest soule indeed. It should be like the* Never-too-well read Arcadia, *where the* Prose *and* Verce, (Matter *and* Words) *are like his* Mistresses *eyes, one still excelling another and without Corivall; or to come home to the vulgars* Element, *like* Friendly Shake-speares Tragedies, *where the* Commedian *rides, when the* Tragedian *stands on Tip-toe. Faith it should please all, like Prince* Hamlet. *But in sadnesse, then it were to be feared he would runne mad. Insooth I will not be moon-sicke to please, nor out of my wits though I displeased all. What? Poet, are you in Passion, or out of Love? This is as* Strange *as* True. *Well, well, if I seeme misticall, or tyrannicall, whether I be a* Foole *or a* Lords-Ingle, *alls one. If you be angry, you are not well advised. I will tell you, tis an Indian* Humour, *I have snuft up from divine* Tabacco; *and tis most Gentleman-like to puffe it out at any place or person. Ile no* Epistle, (*it were worse then one of* Hercules *Labours*) *but will conclude, honesty is a mans best vertue. And but for the* Lord Mayor, *and the two* Sheriffes, *the Innes of Court, and many Gallants elsewhere, this last yeare might have bene burned. As for* Momus, *Carpe and Barke who will, if the* Noble Asse *bray not, I am as good a Knight Poet, as* Etatis suæ, *Maister* An. Dom. *Sonne in Law. Let your* Cryticke *looke to the Rowels of his spurs, the pad of his Saddle, and the Jerke of his Wand; then let him ride me and my Rimes as hotely as he would ride his Mistresse, I care not. We shall meete and be friends againe, with the breaking of a Speare or two. And who would do lesse, for a faire Lady? There I leave you, where you shall ever finde me.*

Passionate Daiphantus: *Your loving* Subject,

Gives you to understand, He is A man in Print, *and tis enough he hath under-gone a* Pressing (*yet not like a* Ladie) *though for your sakes and for* Ladyes, *protesting for this poore Infant of his*

Brayne, as it was the price of his Virginitie borne into the world in teares; so (but for a many his deare friends that tooke much paines for it) it had dyed, and never bene laught at; and that if Truth *have wrote lesse than* Fixion, *yet tis better to erre in Knowledge then in Judgment. Also if he have caught up half a Line of any others, it was out of his* Memorie *not of any ignorance. Why, he Dedicates it to all, and not to any Particular, as his* Mistresse, *or So? His answere is, he is better Borne, than to creepe into* Womens Favours, *and aske their leave afterwards. Also he desireth you to helpe Correct such errors of the Printer, which because the* Authour *is dead (or was out of the Citie) hath beene committed. And twas his folly, or the* Stationers, *you had not an* Epistle *to the purpose.*

Thus like a Lover, wooes he for your Favor,
Which if You grant then *Omnia vincit Amor.*

Francis Bacon, *The Proficience and Advancement of Learning. The First Book*, 1605.

To the King

THERE were under the Lawe (excellent King) both dayly Sacrifices, and free will Offerings; the one proceeding upon ordinarie observance; the other uppon a devout cheerefulnesse. In like manner, there belongeth to Kings from their Servants, both Tribute of dutie and presents of affection. In the former of these, I hope I shal not live to be wanting, according to my most humble dutie, and the good pleasure of your Majesties employments: for the later, I thought it more respective to make choyce of some oblation, which might rather referre to the proprietie and excellencie of your individuall person, than to the business of your Crowne and State.

Wherefore representing your Majestie many times unto my mind, and beholding you not with the inquisitive eye of presumption, to discover that which the Scripture telleth me is inscrutable; but with the observant eye of dutie and admiration: leaving aside the other parts of your vertue and fortune, I have been touched, yea and possessed with an extreame woonder at those your vertues and faculties, which the Philosophers call intellectual: the largenesse of your capacitie, the faithfulnesse of your memorie, the swiftnesse of your apprehension, the penetration of your Judgement, and the facilitie and order of your elocution: and I have often thought, that of all the persons living, that I have knowne, your Majestie were the best instance to make a man of *Plato's* opinion, that all knowledge is but remembrance, and that the minde of man by nature knoweth all things, and hath but her owne native and originall notions (which by the strangenesse and darkenesse of this Tabernacle of the bodie are sequestred) againe revived and restored: such a light of Nature I have observed in your Majestie, and such a readinesse to take flame, and blaze from the least occasion presented, or the least sparke of anothers knowledge delivered. And as the Scripture sayth of the wisest King: *That his heart was as the sands of the Sea;* which though it be one of the largest bodies, yet it consisteth of the smallest & finest portions. So hath God given your Majestie a composition of understanding admirable, being able to compasse & comprehend the greatest matters, & neverthelesse to touch and apprehend the least; whereas it should seeme an impossibility in Nature, for the same Instrument to make it selfe fit for great and small workes. And for your gift of speech, I call to minde what *Cornelius Tacitus* sayth of *Augustus Caesar; Augusto profluens, et quæ principem deceret, eloquentia fuit;* for if we note it well, speech that is uttered with labour and difficultie, or speech that savoureth of the affectation of art and precepts, or speech that is framed after the imitation of some patterne of eloquence, though never so excellent: all this hath somewhat servile, and holding of the subject. But your Majesties manner of speech is indeed Prince-like, flowing as from a fountaine, and yet streaming & branching it selfe into Natures order, full of facilitie & felicitie, imitating none & inimitable by any. And as in your civile Estate there appeareth to be an emulation & contention of your Majesties vertue with your fortune, a vertuous disposition with a fortunate regiment, a vertuous expectation (when time was) of your greater fortune, with a prosperous possession thereof in the due time; a vertuous observation of the lawes of marriage, with most blessed and happy fruite of marriage; a vertuous and most christian desire of peace, with a fortunate inclination in your neighbour Princes thereunto; so likewise in these intellectuall matters, there seemeth to be no lesse contention betweene the excellencie of your Majesties gifts of Nature and the universalitie and profection of your learning. For I am well assured, that this which I shall say is no amplification at all, but a positive and measured truth; which is, that there hath not beene since Christs time any King or temporall Monarch which hath ben so learned in all literature & erudition, divine & humane. For let a man seriously & diligently revolve and peruse the succession of the Emperours of Rome, of which *Caesar* the Dictator, who lived some yeeres before Christ, and *Marcus Antoninus* were the best learned; and so descend to the Emperours of *Grecia,* or of the West, and then to the lines of Fraunce, Spaine, England, Scotland, and the rest, and he shall finde this judgement is truly made. For it seemeth much in a King, if by the compendious extractions of others mens wits and labours, he can take hold of any superficial Ornaments and shewes of learning, or if he countenance and preferre learning and learned men. But to drinke indeed of the true Fountaines of learning, nay, to have such a fountaine of learning in himselfe, in a King, and in a King borne, is almost a Miracle. And the more, because there is met in your Majesty a rare Conjunction, as well of divine and sacred literature, as of prophane and humane; so as your Majestie standeth invested of that triplicitie, which in great veneration, was ascribed to the ancient *Hermes;* the power and fortune of a King; the knowledge and illumination of a Priest; and the learning and universalitie of a Philosopher. This propriety inherent and individuall attribute in your Majestie deserveth to be expressed, not onely in the fame and admiration of the present time, nor in the Historie or tradition of the ages succeeding; but also in some solide worke, fixed memoriall, and immortall monument, bearing a Character or signature, both of the power of a king, and the difference and perfection of such a King.

Therefore I did conclude with myself, that I could not make unto your Majesty a better oblation, then of some treatise tending to that end, whereof the summe will consist of these two partes: the former concerning the excellencie of learning and knowledge, and the excellencie of the merit and true glory, in the Augmentation and Propagation thereof; the latter, what the particular actes and workes are, which have been embraced and undertaken for the advancement of learning: and againe what defects and undervalewes I finde in such particuler actes: to the end, that though I cannot positively or affirmativelie advise your Majestie, or propound unto you framed particulers; yet I may excite your princely Cogitations to visit the excellent treasure of your owne mind, and thence to extract particulers for this purpose, agreeable to your magnanimitie and wiesdome.

Ben Jonson, *Sejanus, His Fall,* 1605.

To the Readers.

THE following and voluntary Labours of my Friends, prefixt to my Booke, have releived me in much whereat (without them) I should necessarilie have touchd. Now I will onely use three of foure short and needfull Notes, and so rest.

First, if it be objected that what I publish is no true *Poëme* in the strict Lawes of *Time,* I confesse it, as also in the want of a proper *Chorus,* whose Habite and Moodes are such and so difficult as not any whome I have seene since the *Auntients* (no, not they who have most presently affected Lawes) have yet come in the way off. Nor is it needful, or almost possible, in these our Times, and to such Auditors as commonly Things are presented, to observe the ould state and splendour of *Drammatick Poëmes,* with preservation of any popular delight. But of this I shall take more seasonable cause to speake in my Observations upon *Horace* his *Art* of *Poetry,* which, with the Text translated, I intend shortly to publish. In the meane time, if in truth of Argument, dignity of Persons, gravity and height of Elocution, fulnesse and frequencie of Sentence, I have discharg'd the other offices of a *Tragick* writer, let not the absence of these *Formes* be imputed to me, wherein I shall give you occasion hereafter (and without my boast) to thinke I could better prescribe then omit the due use for want of a convenient knowledge.

The next is, least in some nice nostrill the *Quotations* might savour affected, I doe let you know that I abhor nothing more, and have onely done it to shew my integrity in the *Story,* and save my selfe in those common Torturers that bring all wit to the Rack, whose Noses are ever like Swine spoyling and rooting up the *Muses* Gardens, and their whole Bodies like Moles, as blindly working under Earth to cast any, the least, hilles upon *Vertue.*

Whereas they are in *Latine,* and the worke in *English,* it was presupposd none but the Learned would take the paynes to conferre them; the Authors themselves being all in the learned *Tongues,* save one, with whose English side I have had little to doe: to which it may be required, since I have quoted the Page, to name what Editions I follow'd: *Tacit. Lips. in 4°, Antwerp. edit. 600. Dio. Folio, Hen. Step. 92.* For the rest, as *Sueton. Seneca,* &c. the Chapter doth sufficiently direct, or the Edition is not varied.

Lastly, I would informe you, that this Booke, in all numbers, is not the same with that which was acted on the publike Stage; wherein a second Pen had good share: in place of which, I have rather chosen to put weaker and, no doubt, lesse pleasing, of mine own, then to defraud so happy a *Genius* of his right by my lothed usurpation.

Fare you well, and if you read farder of me, and like, I shall not be afraid of it, though you praise me out.

Neque enim mihi cornea fibra est.

But that I should plant my felicity in your generall saying, *Good,* or *Well,* &c. were a weaknesse which the better sort of you might worthily contenme, if not absolutely hate me for.

BEN. JONSON. and no such.

Quem Palma negata macrum, donata reducit opimum.

Thomas Dekker, *Newes From Hell*, 1606.

To my most respected, loving, and Juditious friend Mr. John Sturman Gentleman.

SIR, the begetting of Bookes, is as common as the begetting of Children; onely heerein they differ, that Bookes speake so soone as they come into the world, and give the best wordes they can to al men, yet are they driven to seek abroad for a father. That hard fortune follows al & fals now upon THIS of mine. It gladly comes to you upon that errand, and if you vouchsafe to receive it lovingly, I shall account my selfe and It, very happie. Theise Paper-monsters are sure to be set uppon, by many terrible encounters. They had neede therefore to get Armour of proofe that may not shrinke for a bullet. The strongest shieldes that I know for such fights are good Patrons from whom writers claime such antient priviledges, that how-soever they finde entertainment, they make bold to take acquaintance of them (though never so meerely strangers), without blushing: wherein they are like to courtiers, that invite themselves, unbidden, to other mens tables, & that's a most Gentleman-like quality; and yet holde it a disgrace, if they receive not a complementall welcome. Custome making that shew handsomly, which (if the curious handle of Formality, should apparell) would appeare vile Fashion therefore is the best Painter, for what pictures soever she draws, are workmanly done: presuming upon whose warrant, I send unto you the discovery of a strange country. If it were of both Indyes, my love could bestow it upon you. Accept it therefore, and if hereafter I may be a voyager to any happyer coast, the Fruits of (that as now of this) shall be most affectionately consecrated to you.

From him that wishes he could
be a deserver of you.
Tho. Dekker.

Michael Drayton, *Poemes, Lyrick and Pastorall,* 1606(?).

To the deserving memory of my Most esteemed Patron and friend,

Sir Walter Aston, *Knight of the honorable order of the Bath: As before other of my labours, so likewise I consecrate these my latest few Poemes.*

To the Reader.

ODES I have called these the first of my fewe Poems, which how happy soever they proove, yet *Criticism* it selfe cannot saye that the name is wrongfully usurped. For (not to begin with definitions against the rule of oratory, nor *ab ovo,* against the prescript of Poetry in a poeticall argument, but somewhat onely to season thy pallat with a slight description) an Ode is knowne to have been properly a song moduled to the ancient harp, and neither too short breathed as hasting to the end, nor composed of longest verses as unfitte for the suddaine turnes and lofty tricks with which *Apollo* used to menage it. They are (as the learned say) diverse, some transcendently lofty and farre more high then the Epick (commonly called the Heroique Poeme) witnesse those of the Inimitable *Pindarus,* consecrated to the glory and renown of such as returnd in triumph from *Olim-*

pus, Elis, Isthmus or the like. Others among the Greekes are amorous soft and made for chambers, as other for Theaters, as were *Anacreon's* the very delicacies of the Grecian *Erato,* which muse seemed to have beene the mineon of that Teian oulde man which composed them: of a mixd kind were *Horaces* & may truly therefore be called his mixd, whatsoever els are mine little partaking of the hy dialect of the first:

Though we be all to seeke,
Of Pindar *that great Greek*

Nor altogether of *Anacreon,* the arguments being amorous, morrall, or what els the muse pleaseth. To write much in this kind neither know I how it will relish, nor in so doing can I but injuriously presuppose ignorance or sloth in thee, or draw censure upon my selfe for sinning against the *decorum* of a preface, by reading a lecture where it is inough to sum the points. New they are, and the work of playing howers; but what other commendation is theirs, & whether inherent in the subject, must be thine to judge. But to act the go-betweene of my Poems and thy applause, is neither my modesty nor confidence, that oftner then once have acknowledged thee kind, and do not doubt hereafter to do somwhat in which I shall not feare thee just; and would at this time also gladly let thee understand, what I thinke above the rest of the last Ode of the twelve, or if thou wilt Ballad in my Book; for both the great master of Italian rymes *Petrarch,* & our *Chawcer* & other of the uper house of the muses, have thought their Canzons honoured in the title of a Ballade, which for that I labour to meet truely therein with the ould English garb, I hope as able to justifie as the learned *Colin Clout* his Roundelaye. Thus requesting thee in thy better judgement, to correct such faults as have escaped in the printing, I bid thee farewell.

John Marston, *Sophonisba,* 1606.

To the generall Reader.

KNOW, that I have not labored in this poeme, to tie my selfe to relate any thing as an historian but to inlarge every thing as a Poet. To transcribe Authors, quote authorities, & translate Latin prose orations into English blank-verse, hath in this subject, beene the least aime of my studies. Then, (equall Reader) peruse me with no prepared dislike, and if ought shall displease thee, thanke thyself, if ought shall please thee, thanke not me, for I confesse in this it was not my onely end.

Jo. Marston

John Day, *Law Tricks,* 1608.

The Booke to the Reader.

HONEST *Reader,* by thy patience, this is the first time of our meeting, & it may be the last. That's as we shal agree at parting. Woot buy me? The stationer thankes thee. Woot reade mee? Doe: but picke no more out of me, then he that writ put into me: nor knowe me not better then he that made me. Such Mechanicke gods this hil of *Pernassus* harbors. We have a strange secte of upstart *Phisiognomers* growne up amongst us of late, that will assume out of the depth of their knowings, to calculate a mans intent by the colour of his complexion: nay, which is miraculous, by the character of his reporte. And tis wonderfull to consider. Cannot an honest man speake to a knave, but his language must needes be scand? A gallant to a Countrieman, but his intent must be to rob? Must a cucckold of consequent necessitie dwell at the Harts-horne? And a Musitian at the Cat & the fidle? Strange interpretations! I say no more, but if the Cobler wold look no further then the shoe-latchet, we should not have so many corrupt translations. For mine owne part, I reverence all modest advertisements, and submit myselfe to any judicious censurer, protesting I never held any irregular course; but my Inke hath been alwaies simple, without the juice of worm-wood, and my pen smooth, without teeth; and so it shall continue.

Farwell.

Thine or any mans for a testar.

Who would have thought it.

Thomas Heywood, *The Rape of Lucrece*, 1608.

To the Reader.

IT hath beene no custome in mee of all other men (curteous Readers) to commit my plaies to the presse. The reason, though some may attribute to my own insufficiencie, I had rather subscribe, in that, to their seveare censure, then by seeking to avoide the imputation of weakenes, to incurre a greater suspition of honestie; for though some have used a double sale of their labours, first to the Stage, and after to the presse, for my owne part, I heere proclaime my selfe ever faithfull in the first, and never guiltie of the last. Yet since some of my plaies have (unknown to me, and without any of my direction) accidentally come into the Printers handes, and therfore so corrupt and mangled (coppied onely by the eare) that I have bene as unable to know them, as ashamde to chalenge them, this therefore I was the willinger to furnish out in his native habit: first beeing by consent, next because the rest have beene so wronged, in beeing publisht in such savadge and ragged ornaments. Accept it, Curteous Gentlemen, and proove as favourable Readers as wee have found you gratious Auditors.

Yours, *T. H.*

Thomas Middleton, *The Family of Love,* 1608.

To the Reader.

TOO *soone and too late, this work is published: too soone, in that it was in the Presse, before I had notice of it, by which meanes some faults may escape in the Printing: too late, for that it was not published when the general voice of the people had seald it for good, and the newnesse of it made it much more desired, then at this time; for Plaies in this Citie are like wenches new falne to the trade, onelie desired of your neatest gallants, whiles th'are fresh; when they grow stale they must be vented by Termers and Cuntrie chapmen. I know not how this labor will please. Sure I am it past the censure of the Stage with a generall applause, now (whether* vox populi *be* vox dei *or no) that I leave to be tried by the accute judgement of the famous six wits of the Citie: Farewell.*

R. G., *A Good Speed to Virginia*, 1609.

TO THE RIGHT NOBLE AND HONO-RABLE EARLES, BARONS

and Lords, and to the Right Worshipfull Knights, Merchants and Gentlemen, Adventurers for the plantation of *Virginea*, all happie and prosperous successe, which may either augment your glorie, or increase your wealth, or purchase your eternitie.

TIME, the devourer of his own brood, consumes both man and his memorie. It is not brasse nor marble that can perpetuate immortalitie of name upon the earth. Many in the world have erected faire and goodly monuments whose memorie together with their monuments is long since defaced and perished. The name, memorie and actions of those men doe only live in the records of eternitie which have emploied their best endevours in such vertuous and honourable enterprises as have advanced the glorie of God and inlarged the glorie and wealth of their countrie. It is not the house of *Salomon*, called the Forrest of Lebanon, that continues his name and memorie upon the earth at this day, but his wisedome, justice, magnificence and power, yet doe and for ever shall eternize him. A right sure foundation therefore have you (my Lords and the rest of the most worthie Adventurers for Virginia) laid for the immortalitie of your names and memory, which, for the advancement of Gods glorie, the renowne of his Majestie, and the good of your Countrie, have undertaken so honorable a project, as all prosterities shal blesse you, and uphold your names and memories so long as the Sunne and Moone endureth: whereas they which preferre their money before vertue, their pleasure before honour, and their sensuall securitie before heroicall adventures, shall perish with their money, die with their pleasures, and be buried in everlasting forgetfulnes. The disposer of al humane actions dispose your purposes, blesse your Navie, as hee did the ships of *Salomon* which went to Ophie and brought him home in one yeere six hundred threescore and six talents of gold. The preserver of al men preserve your persons from all perils both by sea and land, make your goings out like an host of men triumphing for the victorie, and your commings in like an armie dividing the spoile. And as God hath made you instruments for the inlarging of his Church militant heere upon earth; so when the period of your life shall be finished, the same God make you members of his Church triumphant in Heaven. Amen.

From mine house at the Northend of
Sithes Lane London, April 28.
Anno 1609.

Your Honours and Wor-
ships in all affectionate
well wishing,
R. G.

Richard Hakluyt, *Virginia Richly Valued,* 1609.

TO THE RIGHT HONOURABLE, THE Right Worshipfull Counsellors, and others the cheerefull adventurors for the advancement of that Christian and noble plantation in VIRGINIA.

THIS worke, right Honourable, right Worshipfull, and the rest, though small in shew, yet great in substance, doth yeeld much light to our enterprise now on foot: whether you desire to know the present and future commodities of our countrie; or the qualities and conditions of the Inhabitants, or what course is best to be taken with them.

Touching the commodities, besides the generall report of Cabeça de Vaca *to* Charles *the Emperour (who first travelled through a great part of the Inland of* Florida, *next adjoyning upon our* Virginia) That *Florida* was the richest countrie of the world; and, that after hee had found clothes made of cotton wooll, he saw gold and silver, and stones of great value: *I referre you first to the rich mines of gold reported to be in the province of* Yupaha, *and described in the twelfth Chapter of this Treatise to come within our limits: and againe, to the copper hatchets found in* Cutisachiqui, *standing upon the River of* Santa Helena, *which were said to have a mixture of gold. It seemeth also that the last Chronilcer of the West Indies,* Antonio de Herrera, *speaking of the foresaid River of* Santa Helena, *which standeth in 32. degrees and an halfe, alludeth to the province of* Yupaha, *in these words:* Y el oro, y plata, que hallaron, no era de aquella tierra, sino de 60. leguas adentro al norte, de los pueblos dichos *Otapales* y *Olagatanos,* adonde se intiende, que ay minas de oro, plata, y cobre. *That is to say, That the gold and silver which they found, was not of that countrie* (*of* Santa Helena) *but 60. leagues distant toward the North, of the townes called* Otapales *and* Olagatanos, *where we understand that there are mines of gold, silver, and copper. By which reckoning these rich mines are in the latitude of 35. degrees and an halfe. I desire you likewise to take knowledge of the famous golden province of* Chisca, *stretching further to the North, whereof the Cacique of* Coste *gave notice to* Ferdinando de Soto *in the towne of* Chiaha, *affirming, that there were mines of copper, and of another mettall of the same colour, save that it was finer, and of a farre more perfect lustre, and farre better in sight, and that they used it not so much, because it was softer. And the selfesame thing was before told the Governour in* Cutisachiqui: *who sent two Christians from* Chiaha *with certaine Indians which knew the countrie of* Chisca, *and the language thereof, to view it, and to make report of that which they should finde. We likewise reade not long after, that the Governour set forward to seeke a province called* Pacaha, *which hee was informed to be neere unto* Chisca, *where the Indians told him, that there was gold. And in another place hee saith, that from* Pacaha *hee sent thirtie horsemen and fiftie footmen to the province of* Caluça, *to see if from thence he might travell to*

Chisca, *where the Indians said there was a worke of gold and copper. So that here is foure times mention, and that in sundrie places, of the rich and famous golden mines of* Chisca, *and that they lie beyond the mountaines toward the North, over which they were not able to travell for the roughnes thereof. But what neede I to stand upon forren testimonies, since Master* Thomas Heriot, *a man of much judgement in these causes, signified unto you all, at your late solemne meeting at the house of the right honourable the Earle of Exeter, how to the Southwest of our old fort in* Virginia, *the Indians often informed him, that there was a great melting of red mettall, reporting the manner in working of the same. Besides, our owne Indians have lately revealed either this or another rich mine of copper or gold in a towne called* Ritanoe, *neere certaine mountaines lying West of* Roanoac.

Another very gainfull commoditie is the huge quantitie of excellent perles, and little babies and birds made of them that were found in Cutisachiqui. *The abundance whereof is reported to be such, that if they would have searched divers graves in townes thereabout, they might have laded many of their horses. Neither are the Turkie stones and cotton wooll found at* Guasco *to be forgotten, nor passed over in silence.*

But that, which I make no small account of, is, the multitude of Oxen, which, from the beginning of the 16. to the end of the 26. Chapter, are nine severall times made mention of, and that along from Chiaha, Coste, Pacaha, Coligoa, *and* Tulla, *still toward the North, to wit, toward us, there was such store of them, that they could keepe no corne for them, and that the Indians lived upon their flesh. The haire of these Oxen is likewise said to be like a soft wooll, betweene the course and fine wooll of sheepe: and that they use them for coverlets, because they are very soft and woolled like sheep: and not so onely, but they make bootes, shooes, targets, and other things necessarie of the same. Besides the former benefits, their young ones may be framed to the yoke, for carting and tillage of our ground. And I am in good hope, that ere it be long we shall have notice of their being neerer us, by that which I reade in the Italian relation of* Cabeça de Vaça, *the first finder of them; which writeth,* That they spread themselves within the countrie above foure hundred leagues. *Moreover,* Vasques de Coronado, *and long after him,* Antonio de Espejo (*whose voiages are at large in my third volume*) *travelled many leagues among these heards of Oxen, and found them from 33. degrees ranging very farre to the North and Northeast.*

A fourth chiefe commoditie wee may account to be the great number of Mulberrie trees, apt to feede Silke-wormes to make silke: whereof there was such plentie in many places, that, though they found some hempe in the countrie, the Spaniards made ropes of the barks of them for their brigandines, when they were to put to sea for Noua Hispania.

A fifth is the excellent and perfect colours, as black, white, greene, yellow, and red, and the materials to dye withall, so often spoken of in this discourse: among which I have some hope to bring you to the knowledge of the rich graine of Cochonillio, so much esteemed, and of so great price. I speake nothing of the severall sorts of passing good grapes for Wine and Raisons.

Neither is it the least benefit, that they found salt made by the Indians at Cayas, *and in two places of the province of* Aguacay: *the manner also how the Inhabitants make it is very well worth the observation.*

One of the chiefest of all the rest may be the notice of the South Sea, leading us to Japan *and* China, *which I finde here twice to be spoken of. Whereof long since I have written a discourse, which I thinke not fit to be made over common.*

For closing up this point, the distances of places, the qualities of the soiles, the situations of the regions, the diversities and goodnesse of the fruits, the severall sorts of beasts, the varietie of fowles, the difference betweene the Inhabitants of the mountaines and the plaines, and the riches of the Inland in comparison of the Sea-coast, are judicially set downe in the conclusion of this booke, whereunto for mine owne ease I referre you.

To come to the second generall head, which in the beginning I proposed, concerning the manners and dispositions of the Inhabitants: among other things, I finde them here noted to be very eloquent and well spoken, as the short Orations, interpreted by John Ortiz, *which lived twelve yeeres among them, make sufficient proofe. And the author, which was a gentleman of* Elvas *in* Portugall, *emploied in all the action, whose name is not set downe, speaking of the Cacique of* Tulla, *saith, that aswell this Cacique, as the others, and all those which came to the Governour on their behalfe, delivered their message or speech in so good order, that no Oratour could utter the same more eloquently. But for all their faire and cunning speeches, they are not overmuch to be trusted: for they be the greatest traitors of the world, as their manifold most craftie contrived and bloody treasons, here set down at large, doe evidently prove. They be also as unconstant as the wethercock, and most readie to take all occasions of advantages to doe mischiefe. They are great liars and dissemblers; for which faults often times they had their deserved paiments. And many times they gave good testimonie of their great valour and resolution. To handle them gently, while gentle courses may be found to serve, it will be without comparison the best; but if gentle polishing will not serve, then we shall not want hammerours and rough masons enow, I meane our old soldiours trained up in the Netherlands, to square and prepare them to our Preachers hands. To conclude, I trust by your Honours and Worships wise instructions to the noble Governour, the worthy experimented Lieutenant and Admirall, and other chiefe managers of the businesse, all things shall be so prudently carried, that the painfull Preachers shall be reverenced and cherished, the valiant and forward soldiour respected, the diligent rewarded, the coward emboldened, the weake and sick relieved, the mutinous suppressed, the reputation of the Christians among the Salvages preserved, our most holy faith exalted, all Paganisme and Idolatrie by little and little utterly extinguished. And here reposing and resting my selfe upon this sweete hope, I cease, beseeching the Almightie to blesse this good work in your hands to the honour and glorie of his most holy name, to the inlargement of the dominions of his sacred Majestie, and to the generall good of all the worthie Adventurers and undertakers. From my lodging in the Colledge of Westminster this 15. of Aprill, 1609.*

By one publikely and anciently
devoted to Gods service, and
all yours in this so good action,
Richard Hakluyt.

William Shakespeare, *Troilus and Cressida*, 1609.

A never writer, to an ever reader. Newes.

ETERNALL *reader, you have heere a new play, never stal'd with the Stage, never clapper-clawd with the palmes of the vulger, and yet passing full of the palme comicall; for it is a birth of your braine, that never under-tooke any thing commicall, vainely. And were but the vaine names of commedies changde for the titles of Commodities, or of Playes for Pleas; you should see all those grand censors, that now stile them such vanities, flock to them for the maine grace of their gravities: especially this authors Commedies, that are so fram'd to the life, that they serve for the most common Commentaries, of all the actions of our lives shewing such a dexteritie, and power of witte, that the most displeased with Playes, are pleasd with his Commedies. And all such dull and heavy-witted worldlings, as were never capable of the witte of a Commedie, comming by report of them to his representations, have found that witte there, that they never found in them selves, and have parted better wittied then they came: feeling an edge of witte set upon them, more then ever they dreamd they had braine to grinde it on. So much and such savored salt of witte is in his Commedies, that they seeme (for their height of pleasure) to be borne in that sea that brought forth* Venus. *Amongst all there is none more witty then this. And had*

I time I would comment upon it, though I know it needs not, (for so much as will make you thinke your testerne well bestowd) but for so much worth, as even poore I know to be stuft in it. It deserves such a labour, as well as the best Commedy in Terence *or* Plautus. *And beleeve this, that when hee is gone, and his Commedies out of sale, you will scramble for them, and set up a new English Inquisition. Take this for a warning, and at the perrill of your pleasures losse, and Judgements, refuse not, nor like this the lesse, for not being sullied, with the smoaky breath of the multitude; but thanke fortune for the scape it hath made amongst you; since by the grand possessors wills I beleeve you should have prayd for them rather then beene prayd. And so I leave all such to bee prayd for (for the states of their wits healths) that will not praise it.* Vale.

Thomas Campion, *A New Waye of Making Fowre Partes in Counterpoint,* 1610.

TO THE FLOWRE
OF PRINCES, CHARLES,
PRINCE OF GREAT
BRITTAINE.

THE first inventor of Musicke (most sacred Prince,) was by olde records *Apollo,* a King, who, for the benefit which Mortalls received from his so divine invention, was by them made a God. *David,* a Prophet, and a King, excelled all men in the same excellent Art. What then can more adorne the greatnesse of a Prince, then the knowledge thereof? But why should I, being by profession a Physition, offer a worke of Musicke to his Highnesse? *Galene* either first, or next the first of Physitions, became so expert a Musition, that he could not containe himselfe, but needes he must apply all the proportions of Musicke to the uncertaine motions of the pulse. Such far-fetcht Doctrine dare not I attempt, contenting my selfe onely with a poore, and easie invention; yet new and certaine; by which the skill of Musicke shall be redeemed from much darknesse, wherein envious antiquitie of purpose did involve it. To your gratious hands most humbly I present it, which if your Clemency will vouchsafe favourably to behold, I have then attained to the full estimate of all my labour.

Be all your daies ever musicall (most mighty Prince) and a sweet harmony guide the events of all your royall actions. So zealously wisheth

Your Highnesse
most humble servant,
THO: CAMPION.

Thomas Campion, *A New Waye of Making Fowre Partes in Counterpoint*, 1610.

THE PREFACE.

THERE is nothing doth trouble and disgrace our Traditionall Musition more then the ambiguity of the termes of Musicke, if he cannot rightly distinguish them, for they make him uncapable of any rationall discourse in the art hee professeth. As if wee say a lesser Third consists of a Tone, and a Semi-tone; here by a Tone is ment a perfect Second, or as they name it a whole note. But if wee aske in what Tone is this or that song made, then by Tone we intend the key which guides and ends the whole song. Likewise the word Note *is sometime used proprely, as when in respect of the forme of it, we name it a round or square Note. In regard of the place we say, a Note in rule or a Note in space; so for the time, we call a Briefe or Sembriefe a long Note, a Crotchet or Quaver a short note. Sometime the word* Note *is otherwise to be understood, as when it is,* signum pro signato, *the signe for the thing signified: so we say a Sharpe, or flat Note, meaning by the word Note, the sound it signifies; also we terme a Note high, or low, in respect of the sound. The word* Note *simply produced hath yet another signification, as when we say this is a sweet Note, or the Note I like, but not the words, wee then meane by this word Note, the whole tune, putting the part for the whole. But this word* Note *with addition, is yet far other-*

wise to be understood, as when we say a whole Note, or a halfe Note; we meane a perfect or imperfect Second, which are not Notes, but the severall distances betweene two Notes, the one being double as much as the other; and although this kinde of calling them a whole and a halfe Note, came in first by abusion, yet custome hath made that speech now passable. In my discourse of Musicke, I have therefore strived to be plaine in my tearmes, without nice and unprofitable distinctions, as that is of tonus major, *and* tonus minor, *and such like, whereof there can be made no use.*

In like manner there can be no greater hinderance to him that desires to become a Musition, then the want of the true understanding of the Scale, which proceeds from the errour of the common Teacher, who can doe nothing without the olde Gam-ut, *in which there is but one Cliffe, and one Note, and yet in the same Cliffe he wil sing* re & sol. *It is most true that the first invention of the* gam-ut *was a good invention, but then the distance of Musicke was cancelled within the number of twenty Notes, so were the sixe Notes properly invented to helpe youth in vowelling, but the liberty of the latter age hath given Musicke more space both above and below, altering thereby the former naming of the Notes: the curious observing whereof hath bred much unnecessary difficultie to the learner, for the Scale may be more easily and plainely exprest by foure Notes then by sixe, which is done by leaving out* Ut *and* Re.

The substance of all Musicke and the true knowledge of the scale consists in the observation of the halfe note, which is expressed either by Mi Fa, *or* La Fa, *and they being knowne in their right places, the other Notes are easily applyed unto them.*

To illustrate this I will take the common key which we call

Gam-ut, *both sharpe in* Bemi *and flat, as also flat in* Elami, *and shew how with ease they may be expressed by these foure Notes, which are* Sol, La, Mi, Fa.

I shall neede no more then one eight for all, and that I have chosen to be in the Base, because all the upper eights depend upon the lowest eight, and are the same with it in nature; then thus first in the sharpe:

First observe the places of the halfe Notes which are marked with a halfe circle, and remember that if the lowest be Mi Fa, *the upper halfe Note is* La Fa, *and contrariwise if the lowest halfe Note be* La Fa, *the upper must be* Mi Fa.

It will give great light to the understanding of the Scale, if you trye it on a Lute, or Voyall, for there you shall plainely perceive that there goe two frets to the raising of a whole Note, and but one to a halfe Note, as on the Lute in this manner the former eight may be expressed.

Here you may discerne that betweene A. *and* C. *and* C. *and* E. *is interposed a fret, which makes it double as much as* E. *and* F. *which is markt for the halfe Note, so the whole Note you see containes in it the space of two halfe Notes, as* A.C. *being the whole Note, containes in it these two halfe Notes,* A.B. *and* B.C.

Now for the naming of the Notes, let this be a generall rule, above Fa, *ever to sing* Sol, *and to sing* Sol *ever under* La.

Here in the flat Gam-ut, *you may finde* La Fa *below, and* Mi Fa *above; which on the Lute take their places thus:*

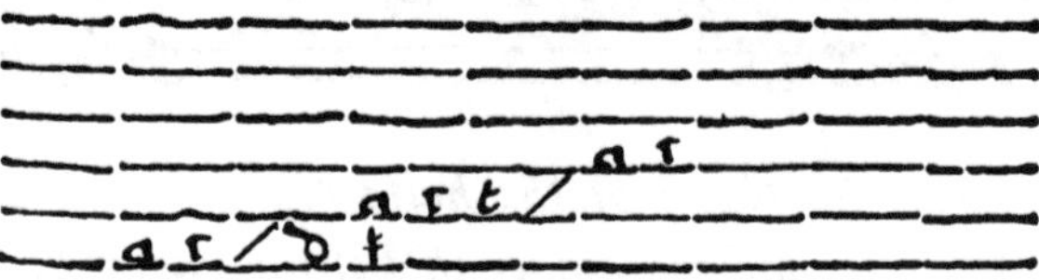

The lower halfe Note is betweene C. *and* D. *the higher betweene* E. *and* A, *but next let us examine this Key as it is flat in* Elami, *which being properly to be set in* Are, *so is it to be sung with ease,* La *instead of* Re, *being the right limits of this eight.*

Mi Fa *here holds his place below, and* La Fa *above but yet removed a Note lower: The same on the Lute.*

You shall here finde the upper halfe Note placed a fret lower then it was in the example of the flat Gam-ut *which was set*

downe next before, by reason of the flat in Elami, *which makes that whole Note but halfe so much as it was being sharpe.*

This is an easie way for him that would eyther with ayde of a teacher, or by his owne industrie learne to sing, and if hee shall well beare in minde the placing of the halfe Notes, it will helpe him much in the knowledge of the cords, which have all their variety from the halfe Note.

John Fletcher, *The Faithful Shepherdess,* c. 1610.

To the Reader.

IF you be not reasonably assurde of your knowledge in this kinde of Poeme, lay downe the booke or read this, which I would wish had bene the prologue. It is a pastorall Tragie-comedie, which the people seeing when it was plaid, having ever had a singuler guift in defining, concluded to be a play of country hired Shepheards, in gray cloakes, with curtaild dogs in strings, sometimes laughing together, and sometimes killing one another; and missing whitsun ales, creame, wassel & morris-dances, began to be angry. In their error I would not have you fall, least you incurre their censure. Understand therefore a pastorall to be a representation of shepheards and shephearddesses, with their actions and passions, which must be such as may agree with their natures, at least not exceeding former fictions, & vulgar traditions. They are not to be adorn'd with any art, but such improper ones as nature is said to bestow, as singing and Poetry, or such as experience may teach them, as the vertues of hearbs & fountaines, the ordinary course of the Sun, moone, and starres, and such like. But you are ever to remember Shepherds to be such, as all the ancient Poets and moderne of understanding have receaved them: that is, the owners of flockes, and not hyerlings. A tragie-comedie is not so called in respect of mirth and killing, but in respect it wants deaths, which is inough to make it no tragedie, yet brings some neere it, which is inough to make it no comedie: which must be a representation of familiar people, with such kinde of trouble as no life be questiond, so that a God is as lawfull in this as in a tragedie, and meane people as in a comedie. Thus much I hope will serve to justifie my Poeme, and make you understand it; to teach you more for nothing, I do not know that I am in conscience bound.

John Fletcher.

Robert Jones, *The Muses Gardin for Delights*, 1610.

To the friendly Censurers.

D*EARE friends, for so I call you, if you please to accept my good meaning, I presented you last with a Dreame, in which I doubt not, but your fantasies have received some reasonable contentment, and now if you please to bee awaked out of that Dreame, I shall for your recreation and refreshing, guide you to the* MUSES GARDEN, *where you shall find such varietie of delights, that questionlesse you will willingly spend some time in the view thereof. In your first entrance into which Garden, you shall meete with Love, Love, and nought but Love, set foorth at large in his colours, by way of decyphering him in his nature. In the midst of it, you shall find Love rejected, upon inconstancie and hard measure of ingratitude. Touching them that are lovers, I leave them to their owne censure in Loves description. And now for the end, it is variable in another maner, for the delight of the eare to satisfie opinion. I am not so arrogant to commend mine owne gifts, neither yet so degenerate, as to beg your tolleration. If these delights of Flowers, or varietie of Fruites, may any wayes be pleasing to your senses, I shall be glad. Otherwise I will vow never to set, sow, plant or graft, and my labours henceforth shall cease to trouble you, if you will needs mislike, I care not. I will prevent your censures, and defie your malice, if you despise me, I am resolute, if you use me with respect, I bid you most heartily*

Farewell.

R. J.

The Holy Bible, Authorized Version or King James' Bible, 1611.

TO THE MOST HIGH AND MIGHTIE Prince, JAMES by the grace of God King of Great Britaine, France and Ireland, Defender of the Faith, &c.

THE TRANSLATORS OF *THE BIBLE,*

wish Grace, Mercie, and Peace, through JESUS

CHRIST *our* LORD.

GREAT and manifold were the blessings (most dread Soveraigne) which Almighty God, the Father of all Mercies, bestowed upon us the people of England, when first he sent your Majesties Royall person to rule and raigne over us. For whereas it was the expectation of many, who wished not well unto our Sion, that upon the setting of that bright *Occidentall Starre* Queene Elizabeth of most happy memory, some thicke and palpable cloudes of darkenesse would so have overshadowed this land, that men should have bene in doubt which way they were to walke, and that it should hardly be knowen, who was to direct the unsetled State. The appearance of your Majestie, as of the *Sunne* in his strength, instantly dispelled those supposed and surmised mists, and gave unto all that were well affected, exceeding cause of comfort; especially when we beheld the government established in your Highnesse and your hopefull Seed, by an undoubted Title, and this also accompanied with Peace and tranquillitie, at home and abroad.

But amongst all our Joyes, there was no one that more filled our hearts, then the blessed continuance of the Preaching of Gods sacred word amongst us, which is that inestimable treasure, which excelleth all the riches of the earth, because the fruit thereof extendeth it selfe, not onely to the time spent in this transitory world, but directeth and disposeth men unto that Eternall happinesse which is above in Heaven.

Then, not to suffer this to fall to the ground, but rather to take it up, and to continue it in that state, wherein the famous predecessour of your Highnesse did leave it; Nay, to goe forward with the confidence and resolution of a man maintaining the trueth of Christ, and propagating it farre and neere, is that which hath so bound and firmely knit the hearts of all your Majesties loyall and Religious people unto you, that your very Name is precious among them, their eye doeth behold you with comfort, and they blesse you in their hearts, as that sanctified person, who under God, is the immediate authour of their true happinesse. And this their contentment doeth not diminish or decay, but every day increaseth and taketh strength, when they observe that the zeale of your Majestie towards the house of God doth not slacke or goe backward, but is more and more kindled, manifesting it selfe abroad in the furthest parts of *Christendome,* by writing in defence of the Trueth, (which hath given such a blow unto that man of Sinne, as will not be healed) and every day at home, by Religious and learned discourse, by frequenting the house of God, by hearing the word preached, by cherishing the teachers therof, by caring for the Church as a most tender and loving nourcing Father.

There are infinite arguments of this right Christian and Religious affection in your Majestie: but none is more forcible to declare it to others, then the vehement and perpetuated desire of the accomplishing and publishing of this Worke which now with all humilitie we present unto your Majestie. For when your Highnesse had once out of deepe judgment apprehended how convenient it was that out of the Originall sacred tongues, together with comparing of the labours, both in our owne and other forreigne Languages of many worthy men who went before us, there should be one more exact Translation of the holy Scriptures into the *English tongue,* your Majestie did never desist to urge and to excite those to whom it was commended, that the worke might be hastened, and that the businesse might be expedited in so decent a maner as a matter of such importance might justly require.

And now at last, by the Mercy of God, and the continuance of our Labours, it being brought unto such a conclusion, as that we have great hope that the Church of *England* shall reape good fruit thereby, we hold it our duety to offer it to your Majestie, not onely as to our King and Soveraigne, but as to the principall moover and Author of the Worke. Humbly craving of your most Sacred Majestie, that since things of this quality have ever bene subject to the censures of ill meaning and discontented persons, it may receive approbation and Patronage from so learned and judicious a Prince as your Highnesse is, whose allowance and acceptance of our Labours, shall more honour and incourage us, then all the calumniations and hard interpretations of other men shall dismay us. So that, if on the one side we shall be traduced by Popish persons at home or abroad, who therefore will maligne us, because we are poore Instruments to make Gods holy Trueth to be yet more and more knowen unto the people whom they desire still to keepe in ignorance and darknesse: or if on the other side, we shall be maligned by selfe-conceited brethren who runne their owne wayes and give liking unto nothing but what is framed by themselves and hammered on their Anvile, we may rest secure, supported within by the trueth and innocencie of a good conscience, having walked the wayes of simplicitie and integritie, as before the Lord; and sustained without, by the powerfull Protection of your Majesties grace and favour, which will ever give countenance to honest and Christian endevours, against bitter censures, and uncharitable imputations.

The Lord of Heaven and earth blesse your Majestie with many and happy dayes, that as his Heavenly hand hath enriched your Highnesse with many singular and extraordinary Graces, so you may be the wonder of the world in this later age, for happinesse and true felicitie, to the honour of that Great God, and the good of his Church, through Jesus Christ our Lord and onely Saviour.

(·.·)

Thomas Coryate, *Crudities*, 1611.

TO THE HIGH
AND MIGHTY PRINCE
HENRY, PRINCE OF WALES,
Duke of Cornwall and Rothsay, Earle
of Chester, Knight of the most
noble Order of the
Garter, &c.

THOUGH *I am very confidently perswaded* (*most gracious Prince, the Orient Pearle of the Christian world*) *that I shall expose my selfe to the severe censure at the least, if not the scandalous calumniations of divers carping criticks, for presuming to dedicate to your Highnesse the greene fruits of my short travels, especially since I am no schollar, but a man altogether unworthy to be dignified with so laudable a title: yet there are some few reasons that have emboldned and encouraged me to present these my silly Observations unto your Highnesse, whereof these two are the chiefest. First, that if your Highnesse will deigne to protect them with your favourable and gracious Patronage, as it were with the seven-fold shield of* Ajax, *or the* ægis *of* Pallas (*a favour that I most humbly crave at your Highnesse hands*) *against the envious cavillations of such criticall Momi as are wont to traduce the labours of other men; it may perhaps yeeld some litle encouragement to many noble and generose yong Gallants that follow your Highnesse Court, and give attendance upon your Peerlesse person, to travell into forraine countries, and inrich themselves partly with the observations, and partly with the languages of outlandish regions, the principall meanes (in my poore opinion) to grace and adorne those courtly Gentlemen, whose noble parentage, ingenuous education, and vertuous conversation have made worthy to be admitted into your Highnesse Court: seeing thereby they will be made fit to doe your Highnesse and their Country the better service when opportunity shall require. For the description of many beautifull Cities, magnificent Palaces, and other memorable matters that I have observed in my travels, may infuse (I hope) a desire to them to travel into transmarine nations, and to garnish their understanding with the experience of other countries. Secondly, because amongst other things that I exhibite in this my Journall to your Princelie view, that most glorious, renowned, and Virgin Citie of Venice, the Queene of the Christian world, that Diamond set in the ring of the Adriatique gulfe, and the most resplendent mirrour of Europe, I have more particularly described, then it hath been ever done before in our English tongue. The description of which famous Citie (were it done with such a curious and elegant stile as it doth deserve) I dare boldly say is a subject worthy for the greatest Monarch in the world to reade over. But for mine owne part I am no schollar (as I have already said) and therefore unable to delineate & paint out the singular beauty thereof in her genuine colours with such an exquisite pensill as an eloquent historiographer ought to doe. Notwithstanding those Observations that I gathered thereof during the time of my aboade there* (*which was about the space of sixe weekes*) *I have written though not as eloquently as a learned traveller would have done, yet as faithfully and truly as any man whatsoever; being often holpen both by the discourse of learned men, and certaine Latin bookes that I found in Italie, wherehence* (*I confesse*) *I derived many principall notes, with which I have beautified the description of many other Italian Cities.*

But me thinks I seeme to heare some Momus objecting unto me now I speake thus of Venice, that this is Crambe bis cocta, *as it is in the proverbe. For we have the historie of Venice* (*he will perhaps say*) *already translated out of Italian into English. Therefore what neede we more descriptions of that Citie? Truly I confesse that Cardinal* Contarens *Commonwealth of Venice hath beene so elegantly translated into English, that any judicious Reader may by the reading thereof much instruct himselfe with the forme of the Venetian governement. But that booke reporteth not halfe so many remarkable matters as mine doth* (absit dicto invidia) *of the antiquities and monuments of that famous Citie, together with the description of Palaces, Churches, the Piazza of* S. Marke, *which is one of the most beautifull places* (*I beleeve*) *that ever was built in any Citie whatsoever of the whole world, and other memorable things of no meane importance. Howbeit were this true that the historie of Venice hath been more then once divulged in our mother tongue, yet I hope your Highnesse will not miscensure me for communicating to my country new notes of this noble City, with a corollarie of Observations that* (*I am sure*) *were never before printed in England, seeing* (*according to the old speech*) δὶς καὶ τρὶς τὰ καλά.

Howsoever, if the curious Reader that is wholy addicted unto novelties, will not so well accept my notes of Venice, for that the historie of the Venetian commonwealth hath beene already printed in our language: neverthelesse I conceive some hope that the descriptions of other Cities which I survayed in divers countries in my travels, as in France, Italie, Switzerland, and some parts of high Germanie, will yeeld more matter of newes unto him, because none of these Cities have beene described in our language that I could ever heare of. And whereas I have written more copiously of the Italian, Helveticall, and German Cities, then of the French, that is to be attributed partly to my industrie (whatsoever the same was) which I used more in Italie, Switzerland, and Germany by many degrees then in France; being often disswaded by some of my fellow travellers from gathering any Observations at all till I came into Italie: and partly to the helpes of bookes which I found in Italie and Germanie, wherewith I have something inlarged the descriptions of those Cities. For seeing I made very short aboade in divers faire Italian Cities, as Cremona, Mantua, &c. (where I desired to have observed al the principall matters thereof) and thereby was barred of opportunity to note such things at large as were most memorable; I held it expedient to borrow some few notes from a certaine Latin booke printed in Italie, rather then to write so briefly of the same, as the shortnesse of time would not otherwise permit me. The like I did in Germanie, being sometimes beholding to Munster *for some speciall matter which neither by my owne Observations, nor by the discourse of learned men I could attaine unto, especially about the institution of the Bishopricks of certaine Cities through the which I passed.*

I meant to have digressed into the praise of the excellency of travell into forraine countries, the more to stirre up yong Gentlemen and every good spirit that favours learning to so worthy an exercise; had I not prevented my selfe by translating those two elegant Orations out of Latin into English that were made by that learned German Hermannus Kirchnerus *of Marpurg, which I have inserted into my Booke, the one in commendation of travell in generall, the other of Germanie in particular, which are seasoned with such savourie Attick conceits, and adorned with those* flosculi & pigmenta eloquentiæ, *that I may fitly apply unto them that prety Distiche of the Poet Lucilius:*

> Quàm lepidè lexeis compostæ, ut tesserulæ, omnes
> Arte pavimento, atque emblemate vermiculato.

And surely for my owne part I will say I never read any orations in all my life composed with a more terse and polished stile (Tullies *only excepted*) *though I have in my daies perused some part of the Orations of learned* Melancthon, *the* Phœnix *of Germanie,* Antonie Muretus, *my owne Rhetoricall countryman,* Robert Turner, *&c. Therefore since these two Orations do yeeld stronger motives, and more forceable arguments to animate the learned to travell into outlandish regions, then my poore invention can affoord, I have thought fit to turne them into our mother tongue, according to my simple skill, and to present them also to your Highnesse, together with the Observations of my travels; both because I hope they will be very delectable to every Reader that loveth to heare of forraine affaires, and also for that they agree with the argument of my booke.*

As for these my Observations in forraine countries, I was so farre from presuming to dedicate them to your Highnesse before the consummation of my future travels, that I resolved rather to conceale them from the world, and to bury them for a time in oblivion, if the importunity of some of my deare friends had not prevailed with me for divulging the same: whereof one amongst the rest, namely that right worshipfull Gentleman, my most sincere and entire friend, M. Lionel Cranfield *was the originall and principall animator of me; and another of my friends, even learned* M. Laurence Whitaker, *that elegant Linguist and worthy traveller, now Secretarie to my illustrious* Mecœnas, *Sir* Edward Philips, *Master of the Rolles, hath often urged unto me that proverbiall verse:*

πολλὰ μεταξὺ πέλει κύλικος καὶ χείλεος ἄκρου.

By which he signified that many sinister accidents might happen unto me betwixt the time of my next going out of England, and my arrivall againe in my country; and so consequently my friends and country might be deprived of the fruits of my past travels, and of those to come: by these and such like perswasions of my friends I was animated to publish the Observations of my travels much sooner then I thought to have done, and to addresse them to your excellent Highnesse; not that I hold them worthy to undergoe your Highnesse censure, seeing many of them deserve rather ad salsamantarios amandari, *as learned* Adrian Turnebus *writeth of his* Adversaria, *and* (*as* Horace *saith:*)

Deferri in vicum vendentem thus & odores,
Et piper, & quicquid chartis amicitur ineptis.

but because they shall be an introduction (*if your Highnesse will vouchsafe to Patronize them with your Princely protection*) *to farre more memorable matters that I determine by Gods gracious indulgence to observe hereafter in most of the famous Cities and Princes Courts of Germanie and Italie: as also in Constantinople, with divers ancient Cities of Greece, and the holy Land, as Jeru-*

salem, Jericho, Samaria, and other sacred places mentioned in the Scriptures, and celebrated for the miracles done therein by our blessed Saviour. Of which Cities (if God shall grant me a prosperous issue to my designements) I hope to write after a more particular manner then any of our English travellers have done before me. Wherefore most humbly beseeching your Highnesse to pardon my presumption, I recommend your Highnesse to the mercifull clientele of him whose throne is the heaven, and whose foote-stoole is the earth.

By him

That travelleth no lesse in all humble and dutifull observance to your Highnesse then he did to Venice and the parts above mentioned,

Your Highnesse poore Observer,

THOMAS CORYATE,

Peregrine of Odcombe.

Francis Beaumont, *The Masque of the Inner-Temple & Gray's Inn*, 1612.

TO THE WORTHIE SIR FRANCIS BACON, HIS MAJESTIES SOLLICITOR GENErall, and the grave and learned Bench of the anciently allied houses of Grayes Inne, and the Inner Temple, the Inner *Temple, and Grayes Inne.*

Y*EE that spared no time nor travell, in the setting forth, ordering, & furnishing of this Masque, being the first fruits of honor in this kinde, which these two societies have offered to his Majestie, will not thinke much now to looke backe upon the effects of your owne care and worke: for that whereof the successe was then doubtfull, is now happily performed and gratiously accepted and that which you were then to thinke of in straites of time, you may now peruse at leysure. And you, Sir* Francis Bacon, *especially, as you did then by your countenance and loving affection advance it, so let your good word grace it and defend it, which is able to adde value to the greatest, and least matters.*

George Chapman, *The Widdowes Teares*, 1612.

To the right Vertuous and truly *noble Gentleman,* Mr. Jo. Reed of Mitton, in the Countie of Glo-cester, Esquire.

SIR, *if any worke of this nature be worth the presenting to Friends Worthie, and Noble; I presume this will not want much of that value. Other Countrie men have thought the like worthie of Dukes and Princes acceptations;* Injusti Sdegnij; Il Pentamento Amorose; Calisthe, Pastor Fido, &c. (*all being but plaies*) *were all dedicate to Princes of Italie. And, therefore, only discourse to shew my love to your right vertuous and noble disposition, this poor Comedie* (*of many desired to see printed*) *I thought not utterly unworthie that affectionate designe in me. Well knowing that your free judgement weighs nothing by the Name, or Forme; or any vaine estimation of the vulgar; but will accept acceptable matter, as well in Plaies; as in many lesse materialls, masking in more serious Titles. And so, till some worke more worthie I can select, and perfect, out of my other Studies, that may better expresse me; and more fit the gravitie of your ripe inclination, I rest,*

Yours at all parts most truly affected,

Geo. Chapman.

Nathaniel Field, *A Woman is a Weathercock*, 1612.

To any Woman that hath beene no Weather-Cocke.

I *DID determine, not to have Dedicated my Play to any Body, because forty shillings I care not for, and above, few or none will bestowe on these matters, especially falling from so famelesse a pen as mine is yet. And now I looke up, and finde to whom my Dedication is, I feare I am as good as my determination: notwithstanding, I leave a libertie to any Lady or woman, that dares say she hath beene no weather-Cocke, to assume the Title of Patronesse to this my Booke. If she have beene constant, and be so, all I will expect from her for my paynes, is that she will continue so, but till my next Play be printed, wherein she shall see what amendes I have made to her, and all the sex, and so I end my Epistle, without a Latine sentence.*

N. F.

Nathaniel Field, *A Woman is a Weathercock*, 1612.

TO THE READER.

READER, the Sale-man sweares youle take it very ill, if I say not somewhat to you too. Introth, you are a stranger to me; why should I Write to you? You never writ to mee, nor I thinke will not answere my Epistle. I send a Comedie to you heer, as good as I could then make; nor sleight my presentation, because it is a play: For I tell thee Reader, if thou bee'st ignoraunt, a Play is not so ydle a thing as thou art, but a Mirrour of mens lives and actions now, be it perfect or imperfect, true or false, is the Vice or Vertue of the Maker. This is yet, as well, as I can, *Qualeis ego vel Cluvienus.* Thou must needs have some other Language then thy Mother tong, for thou thinkst it impossible for me to write a Play that did not use a word of Latine though he had enough in him. I have beene vexed with vile playes my selfe, a great while, hearing many, nowe I thought to be even with some, and they shoulde heare mine too. Fare thee well, if thou hast any thing to say to me, thou know'st where to heare of me for a yeare or two, and no more I assure thee.

N. F.

Thomas Heywood, *An Apology for Actors*, 1612.

To my good Friends and Fellowes the Citty-Actors.

O*UT of my busiest houres, I have spared my selfe so much time as to touch some particulars concerning us, to approve our Antiquity, ancient Dignity, and the true use of our quality. That it hath beene ancient, we have derived it from more then two thousand yeeres agoe, successively to this age. That it hath beene esteemed by the best and greatest: to omit all the noble Patrons of the former world, I need alledge no more then the Royall and Princely services, in which we now live. That the use thereof is authentique, I have done my endeavour to instance by History, and approve by authority. To excuse my ignorance in affecting no florish of Eloquence, to set a glosse upon my Treatise, I have nothing to say for my selfe but this:* A good face needs no painting & a good cause no abetting. *Some over-curious have too liberally taxed us: and hee (in my thoughts) is held worthy reproofe, whose ignorance cannot answere for it selfe: I hold it more honest for the guiltlesse to excuse, then the envious to exclaime. And we may as freely (out of our plainnesse) answere, as they (out of their perversnesse object) instancing my selfe by famous* Scalliger, *learned Doctor* Gager, *Doctor* Gentiles, *and others, whose opinions and approved arguments on our part, I have in my briefe discourse altogether omitted; because I am loath to bee* *taxed in borrowing from others: and besides, their workes being extant to the world, offer themselves freely to every mans perusall. I am profest adversary to none, I rather covet reconcilement, then opposition, nor proceedes this my labour from any envy in me, but rather to shew them wherein they erre. So wishing you judiciall Audiences, honest Poets, and true gatherers, I commit you all to the fulnesse of your best wishes.*

Yours ever,

T. H.

Thomas Heywood, *An Apology for Actors*, 1612.

TO THE JUDICIALL READER.

I HAVE undertooke a subject (courteous Reader) not of sufficient countenance to bolster it selfe by his owne strength; and therefore have charitably reached it my hand to support it against any succeeding Adversary. I could willingly have committed this worke to some more able then my selfe: for the weaker the Combatant, hee needeth the stronger Armes. But in extremities, I hold it better to weare rusty Armour, then to goe naked; yet if these weake habilliments of warre, can but buckler it from part of the rude buffets of our Adversaries, I shall hold my paines sufficiently guerdoned. My pen hath seldome appeared in Presse till now, I have beene ever too jealous of mine owne weaknesse, willingly to thrust into the Presse: nor had I at this time, but that a kinde of necessity enjoyned me to so sudden a businesse. I will neither shew my selfe over-presumtuous, in skorning thy favour, nor too importunate a beggar, by too servilly intreating it. What thou art content to bestow upon my pains, I am content to accept: if good thoughts, they are all I desire: if good words, they are more then I deserve: if bad opinion, I am sorry I have incur'd it: if evil language, I know not how I have merited it: if any thing, I am pleased: if nothing, I am satisfied, contenting my selfe with this: I have done no more then (had I beene called to account) shewed what I could say in the defence of my owne quality.

Thine,

T. HEYWOOD.

Firma valent per se, nullumque Machaona quaerunt.

Ben Jonson, *The Alchemist*, 1612.

TO THE READER.

IF thou beest more, thou art an Understander, and then I trust thee. If thou art one that tak'st up, and but a Pretender, beware at what hands thou receiv'st thy commoditie; for thou wert never more fair in the way to be cos'ned (then in this Age) in Poetry, *especially in Playes: wherein, now, the Concupiscence of Jigges and Daunces so raigneth, as to runne away from Nature, and be afraid of her, is the onely point of art that tickles the* Spectators. *But how out of purpose and place doe I name Art? When the Professors are growne so obstinate contemners of it, and presumers on their owne Naturalls, as they are deriders of all diligence that way, and by simple mocking at the termes, when they understand not the things, thinke to get of wittily with their Ignorance. Nay, they are esteem'd the more learned and sufficient for this by the Multitude through their excellent vice of judgement. For they commend Writers as they doe Fencers or Wrastlers; who, if they come in robustuously and put for it with a great deale of violence, are receiv'd for the braver fellowes: when many times their owne rudenesse is the cause of their disgrace, and a little touch of their Adversary gives all that boisterous force the foyle. I deny not but that these men, who alwaies seeke to doe more then inough, may some time happen on some thing that is good and great but very seldome. And when it comes, it doth not recompence the rest of their ill. It sticks out perhaps, and is more eminent, because all is sordide and vile about it, as lights are more discern'd in a thick darknesse then a faint shadow. I speake not this out of a hope to doe good on any man against his will; for I know, if it were put to the question of theirs and mine, the worse would finde more suffrages, because the most favour common errors. But I give thee this warning, that there is a great difference betweene those that (to gain the opinion of Copie) utter all they can, how ever unfitly, and those that use election and a meane. For it is onely the disease of the unskilfull to thinke rude things greater then polish'd, or scatter'd more numerous then compos'd.*

John Webster, *The White Divel*, 1612.

To the Reader.

IN publishing this Tragedy, I do but challenge to my selfe that liberty which other men have tane before mee; not that I affect praise by it, for nos hæc novimus esse nihil; *onely, since it was acted in so dull a time of Winter, presented in so open and blacke a Theater, that it wanted (that which is the onely grace and setting out of a Tragedy) a full and understanding Auditory: and that, since that time, I have noted most of the people that come to that Play-house resemble those ignorant asses (who, visiting Stationers shoppes, their use is not to inquire for good bookes, but new bookes) I present it to the generall veiw with this confidence:*

Nec Ronchos metues maligniorum,
Nec Scombris tunicas dabis molestas.

If it be objected this is no true Drammaticke Poem, I shall easily confesse it, non potes in nugas dicere plura meas: Ipse ego quam dixi, *willingly, and not ignorantly, in this kind have I faulted: for should a man present to such an Auditory the most sententious Tragedy that ever was written, observing all the critticall lawes, as heighth of stile and gravety of person, inrich it with the sententious* Chorus, *and, as it were, life'n Death in the passionate and waighty* Nuntius; *yet, after all this divine rapture,* O dura messorum ilia, *the breath that comes from the uncapable multitude is able to poison it; and ere it be acted, let the Author resolve to fix to every scæne this of* Horace,

—Hæc hodie Porcis comedenda relinques.

To those who report I was a long time in finishing this Tragedy, I confesse I do not write with a goose-quill, winged with two feathers; and if they will needes make it my fault, I must answere them with that of Eurypides *to* Alcestides, *a Tragicke Writer:* Alcestides *objecting that* Eurypides *had onely in three daies composed three verses, whereas himselfe had written three hundreth: Thou telst truth (quoth he) but heres the difference; thine shall onely bee read for three daies, whereas mine shall continue three ages.*

Detraction is the sworne friend to ignorance. For mine owne part, I have ever truly cherisht my good opinion of other mens worthy Labours; especially of that full and haightned stile of Maister Chapman, *the labor'd and understanding workes of Maister* Johnson, *the no lesse worthy composures of the both worthily excellent Maister* Beamont *& Maister* Fletcher, *and lastly (without wrong last to be named) the right happy and copious industry of M.* Shake-speare, *M.* Decker, *& M.* Heywood; *wishing what I write may be read by their light: protesting that, in the strength of mine owne judgement, I know them so worthy, that though I rest silent in my owne worke, yet to most of theirs I dare (without flattery) fix that of* Martiall:

—non norunt Hæc monumenta mori.

Thomas Shelton, *The History of the Valorous and Witty Knight-Errant Don Quixote of the Mancha*, 1612–20. *The First Part.*

To the Right Ho nourable His Verie Good Lord, The Lord of Walden, &C.

MINE Honourable Lord; having Translated some five or sixe yeares agoe, the Historie of *Don Quixote,* out of the Spanish tongue into English, in the space of forty daies; being therunto more then halfe enforced, through the importunitie of a very deere friend, that was desirous to understand the subject: After I had given him once a view thereof, I cast it aside, where it lay long time neglected in a corner, and so little regarded by me, as I never once set hand to review or correct the same. Since when, at the intreatie of others my friends, I was content to let it come to light, conditionally, that some one or other, would peruse and amend the errours escaped; my many affaires hindering mee from undergoing that labour. Now I understand by the Printer, that the Copie was presented to your Honour: which did at the first somewhat disgust mee, because as it must passe, I feare much, it will prove farre unworthy, either of your Noble view or protection. Yet since it is mine, though abortive, I doe humbly intreate, that your Honour will lend it a favourable countenance, thereby to animate the parent thereof to produce in time some worthier subject, in your Honourable name, whose many rare vertues have already rendred me so highly devoted to your service, as I will some day give very evident tokens of the same, and till then I rest,

Your Honours most affectionate
servitor,
Thomas Shelton.

Michael Drayton, *Poly-olbion*, 1612–22.
The First Part, 1612.

TO THE HIGH AND MIGHTIE, *HENRIE*, *Prince of Wales.*

THIS first part of my intended Poeme I consecrate to your Highnes: in whom (beside my particuler zeale) there is a naturall interest in my Worke as the hopefull Heyre of the kingdoms of this Great *Britaine:* whose Delicacies, Chorographicall Description, and Historie, be my subject. My Soule, which hath seene the extremitie of Time and Fortune, cannot yet despaire. The influence of so glorious and fortunate a Starre may also reflect upon me: which hath power to give me new life, or leave me to die more willingly and contented. My Poeme is genuine, and first in this kinde. It cannot want envie: for, even in the Birth, it alreadie finds that. Your Gracious acceptance, mighty Prince, will lessen it. May I breath to arrive at the *Orcades* (whither in this kind I intend my course, if the Muse fail me not) I shall leave your whole British Empire, as this first and southerne part, delineated:

To your HIGHNES,
The most humbly
devoted,
Michael Drayton.

Michael Drayton, *Poly-olbion*, 1612–22.
The Second Part, 1622.

TO THE HIGH AND MIGHTIE, CHARLES, *Prince of WALES.*

THE First Part of this Poeme (most Illustrious Prince) I dedicated to your deceased Brother of most famous Memorie, whose princely Bountie, and usage of mee, gave me much encouragement to goe on with this second Part, or Continuance thereof; which now, as his Successor, I owe to your Highnesse. If meanes and time fail me not, being now arived at Scotland, *I trust you shall see mee crowne her with no worse Flowers, then I have done her two Sisters,* England *and* Wales: *and without any partialitie, as I dare bee bold, to make the Poets of that Kingdom my Judges therin. If I arive at the* Orcades, *without sinking in my flight, your Highnesse cannot but say, that I had no ill Perspective that gave me things so cleerely, when I stood so farre off.*

To your Highnesse
most humbly devoted,
Michael Drayton.

Michael Drayton, *Poly-olbion,* 1612–22.
The Second Part, 1622.

To any that will read it.

WHEN I first undertooke this Poeme, or, as some very skilfull in this kind, have pleased to tearme it, this Herculean labour, I was by some vertuous friends perswaded, that I should receive much comfort and incouragement therein; and for these Reasons: First, that it was a new, cleere way, never before gone by any; then, that it contained all the Delicacies, Delights, and Rarities of this renowned Isle, interwoven with the Histories of the Britanes, Saxons, Normans, and the later English: And further that there is scarcely any of the Nobilitie, or Gentry of this land, but that he is some way or other, by his Blood interressed therein. But it hath fallen out otherwise; for instead of that comfort, which my noble friends (from the freedome of their Spirits) proposed as my due, I have met with barbarous Ignorance, and base Detraction; such a cloud hath the Devill drawne over the World's Judgement, whose opinion is in few yeares fallen so farre below all Ballatry, that the Lethargy is incurable; nay some of the Stationers, that had the Selling of the first part of this Poeme, because it went not so fast away in the Sale, as some of their beastly and abominable Trash, (a shame both to our Language and Nation) have either despightfully left out, or at least carelessely neglected the Epistles to the Readers, and so have cousoned the Buyers with unperfected Bookes; which these that have undertaken the second Part, have beene forced to amend in the first, for the small number that are yet remaining in their hands. And some of our outlandish, unnaturall English, (I know not how otherwise to expresse them) sticke not to say, that there is nothing in this Island worthy studying for, and take a great pride to bee ignorant in any thing thereof; for these, since they delight in their folly, I wish it may be hereditary from them to their posteritie, that their children may bee beg'd for Fooles to the fift Generation, untill it may be beyond the memory of man to know that there was ever any other of their Families: neither can this deterre mee from going on with Scotland, if Meanes and Time doe not hinder me, to performe as much as I have promised in my first Song:

> *Till to the sleepy Maine, to* Thuly *I have gone,*
> *And seene the Frozen Isles, the cold* Deucalidon,
> *Amongst whose iron Rocks, grim* Saturne *yet remaines*
> *Bound in those gloomy Caves with Adamantine Chaines.*

And as for those Cattell whereof I spake before, *Odi profanum vulgus, & arceo,* of which I account them, bee they never so great, and so I leave them. To my friends, and the lovers of my Labors, I wish all happinesse.

Michael Drayton.

Francis Beaumont, *The Knight of the Burning Pestle,* 1613.

To the Readers of this COMEDIE.

G*ENTLEMEN,* the World is so nice in these our times, that for Apparrell, there is no fashion; for Musicke, which is a rare Art (though now slighted) no Instrument; for Diet, none but the *French* Kickshoes that are delicate; and for Playes, no invention but that which now runneth an invective way, touching some particular person, or else it is contemned before it is throughly understood. This is all that I have to say, that the Author had no intent to wrong any one in this *Comedy,* but as a merry passage, here and there interlaced it with delight, which hee hopes will please all, and be hurtfull to none.

John Florio, *Essayes Written in French by Montaigne Done into English*, 1613.

TO THE MOST ROYAL AND RENOWMED

Majestie of the High-Borne Princesse Anna of Denmarke, *By the* Grace of God Queene of *England, Scotland, France,* and *Ireland,* &c.

Imperiall and Incomparable Majestie.

SEEING with me, all of me is in your Royall possession, and whatsoever pieces of mine have heretofore, under other starres passed the publike view, come now of right to be under the predomination of a Power, that both contains all their perfections, and hath influences of a more sublime nature. I could not but also take in this part (wherof time had worn-out the edition) which the world hath long since had of mine, and lay it at your Sacred feet, as a memoriall of my devoted dutie, and to shew that where I am, I must be all I am, and can not stand dispersed in my observance, being wholly (and therein happy)

Your sacred Majesties *most*
humble and loyall servant
John Florio.

John Florio, *Essayes Written in French by Montaigne Done into English*, 1613.

TO THE READER.

ENOUGH, if not too much, hath been sayd of this Translation. If the faults found even by my selfe in the first impression, be now by the Printer corrected, as he was directed, the worke is much amended. If not, know, that through mine attendance on hir Majestie, I could not intend it; and blame not *Neptune* for thy second shipwracke. Let me conclude with this worthie mans daughter of alliance: *Que t'en semble donc lecteur?*

Still resolute John Florio.

Thomas Middleton, *The Witch,* 1613.

To the Truely-Worthie
and
Generously-Affected
THOMAS HOLMES, Esquire.

Noble Sir,

AS a true testemonie of my readie inclination to your service, I have (meerely uppon a tast of your desire) recovered into my hands (though not without much difficultie) this (ignorantly-ill-fated) labour of mine.

Witches are (*ipso facto*) by the law condemn'd, & that onely (I thinck) hath made her lie so long in an imprisond obscuritie. For your sake alone She hath thus far conjur'd herself abroad; and beares noe other charmes about her, but what may tend to your recreation, nor no other spell but to possess you with a belief, that as She, so He that first taught her to enchant, will alwaies be

Your devoted
THO. MIDDLETON

William Browne, *The Inner Temple Masque,* 1614.

To the honorable society of the Inner Temple.

Gentlemen.

I *GIVE you but your owne. If you refuse to foster it, I knowe not who will. By your meanes it may live. If it degenerate in kinde from those other our society hath produced, blame your selves for not seekinge to a happier muse. I knowe it is not without faultes, yet such as your loves, or at least Poetica Licentia (the common salve) will make tollerable. What is good in it, that is yours; what bad, myne; what indifferent, both; & that will suffice, since it was done to please ourselves in private by him that is*

All yours,
W. Browne

John Donne, *Obsequies to the Lord Harrington*, 1614.

To the Countesse of Bedford.

MADAME,

I HAVE learn'd by those lawes wherein I am a little conversant, that hee which bestowes any cost upon the dead, obliges him which is dead, but not the heire; I do not therefore send this paper to your Ladyship, that you should thanke mee for it, or thinke that I thanke you in it; your favours and benefits to mee are so much above my merits, that they are even above my gratitude, if that were to be judged by words which must expresse it. But, Madame, since your noble brothers fortune being yours, the evidences also concerning it are yours, so his vertue being yours, the evidences concerning it, belong also to you, of which by your acceptance this may be one peece, in which quality I humbly present it, and as a testimony how intirely your familie possesseth

Your Ladiships most humble
and thankfull servant
JOHN DONNE.

Barnaby Rich, *The Honestie of This Age,* 1614.

TO THE RIGHT HONORABLE SYR *Thomas Middleton,* Knight, L. *Maior* of the Honorable Cittie of *London.*

MOST Honorable Lord, to avoid idlenes, I have with *Domitian,* endevoured to catch *Flies;* I have taken in hand a text that will rather induce hatred, then winne love. I have spoken against those abhominations that are not lesse odible in the sight of the powers of heaven, then monstrous to bee tollerated heere upon the face of the earth. I have grasped at greater matters, then (some will say), is fitting to be handled by a Souldier's penne.

The *Adulterer* will not indure it, the *Drunkard* wil be angry with it, the *Blasphemer* will sweare at it, the *Bribetaker* will despite it, the *Papist* will malice it. To conclude (most Honorable) there is no guiltie conscience that will willingly entertaine it.

Remayning then in some doubtfulnes of mind to whom I might bequeath it, that would eyther grace or give countenance unto it, I was prompted by *Report* of your Lordships worthinesse, that now in the course of your governement in this Honorable Cittie of *London,* you have set up those lights for the suppressing of severall sorts of sinnes, that as they have already advanced your applause amongst those that bee of the best approoved honesty, so they will remaine for ever in Record to your perpetuall prayse.

Let not, therefore, my boldnes seeme presumptuous that being altogether unknowne to your Lordship, have yet presumed to shelter my lines under your Honorable name, and thus in affiance of your Honorable acceptance, I rest to doe your Lordshippe any other kinde of service.

Your *Lordships* to commaund

Barnabe Rich

Richard Brathwaite, *A Strappado for the Divell*, 1615.

To the gentle Reader.

IF I give thee a deserving Title (Gentle Reader) no question but thou wilt expresse they selfe in thy censure. Th' art no wri-neck critick, politick informer of States, depraver of wel intended lines, nor maligner of others labours. Bee thine owne president in the surveigh of these distempered *Epigrammes;* and therein thou may performe the part of an honest man. Cancell the bill of errours, or chalke them on, & they shal serve to make up a greater volume for next impression. If thou bee gentle (as I tearme thee) and hast sense, thou wilt supplie many defects committed in the *Presse* by the Authors absence. Be honest still and thou art out of the swing of this strappado. If thou play Recreant (by consorting with the swartie miscreants of *Lucifer*), the *Author* hath vowed hee will play Arch-Pyrate with thee, tie thee like a Gallie-slave to the Mast of his *Malu-Sperauza,* and ferrie thee over into *Tartarie.*

Farewell.

George Sandys, *A Relation of a Journey Begun An. Dom. 1610*, 1615.

TO THE PRINCE.

SIR, the Eminence of the degree wherein God and Nature have placed you doth allure the eyes, and the hopefulnesse of your Vertues win the love of all men. For Vertue, being in a private person an exemplary ornament, advanceth it selfe in a Prince to a publike blessing. And as the Sunne to the world, so bringeth it both light and life to a kingdome: a light of derection, by glorious example; and a life of joy, through a gracious government. From the just and serious consideration whereof, there springeth in minds not brutish, a thankfull correspondence of affection and duty; still pressing to expresse themselves in endevours of service. Which also hath caused me, (most noble Prince) not furnished of better meanes, to offer in humble zeale to your princely view these my doubled travels; once with some toyle and danger performed, and now recorded with sincerity and diligence. The parts I speake of are the most renowned countries and kingdomes: once the seats of most glorious and triumphant Empires; the theaters of valour and heroicall actions; the soiles enriched with all earthly felicities; the places where Nature hath produced her wonderfull works; where Arts and Sciences have bene invented, and perfited; where wisedome, vertue, policie, and civility have bene planted, have flourished: and lastly where God himselfe did place his own Commonwealth, gave lawes and oracles, inspired his Prophets, sent Angels to converse with men; above all, where the Sonne of God descended to become man; where he honoured the earth with his beautifull steps, wrought the worke of our redemption, triumphed over death, and ascended into glory. Which countrie once so glorious, and famous for their happy estate, are now through vice and ingratitude, become the most deplored spectacles of extreme miserie: the wild beasts of mankind having broken in upon them, and rooted out all civilitie; and the pride of a sterne and barbarous Tyrant possessing the thrones of ancient and just dominion. Who aiming onely at the height of greatnesse and sensuality, hath in tract of time reduced so great and so goodly a part of the world, to that lamentable distresse and servitude, under which (to the astonishment of the understanding beholders) it now faints and groneth. Those rich lands at this present remaine wast and overgrowne with bushes, receptacles of wild beasts, of theeves and murderers; large territories dispeopled, or thinly inhabited; goodly cities made desolate; sumptuous buildings become ruines; glorious Temples either subverted, or prostituted to impietie; true religion discountenanced and oppressed; all Nobility extinguished; no light of learning permitted, nor Vertue cherished: violence and rapine insulting over all, and leaving no security save to an abject mind, and unlookt on poverty. Which calamities of theirs so great and deserved, are to the rest of the world as threatning instructions. For assistance wherein, I have not onely related what I saw of their present condition; but so far as conveniency might permit, presented a brief view of the former estates, and first antiquities of those peoples and countries; thence to draw a right image of the frailty of man, *and mutability of what so ever is worldly; and assurance that as there is nothing unchangeable saving God,* so nothing *stable but by his grace and protection.* Accept great Prince these weake endevours of a strong desire: which shall be alwaies devoted to do your Highnesse all acceptable service; and ever rejoyce in your prosperity and happinesse.

George Sandys.

George Wither, *The Shepheards Hunting*, 1615.

TO THOSE HONOURED, NOBLE, and right Vertuous Friends, my Visitants in the *Marshalsey.* AND, TO ALL OTHER MY UNKNOWNE FAVOURITES, who either privatly, or publiquely wished me well in my imprisonment.

N*OBLE Friends, you whose vertues made me first in love with Vertue, and whose worths, made me be thought worthy of your loves, I have now at last (you see) by Gods assistance and your encouragement, run through the Purgatorie of imprisonment: and by the worthy favour of a just PRINCE, stand free againe, without the least touch of dejected basenesse. Seeing therefore I was growne beyonde my Hope so fortunate (after acknowledgment of my Creators love, togeather with the unequall'd Clemency of so gracious a Soveraigne) I was troubled to thinke by what meanes I might expresse my thankful-*

nesse to so many well-deserving friends. No way I found to my desire; neither yet abilitie to performe when I found it. But at length considering with my self what you were, (that is) such who favour honestie for no second reason, but because you your selves are good; and ayme at no other reward, but the witnesse of a sound conscience that you doe well, I found, that thankefulnesse would prove the acceptablest present to sute with your dispositions; and that I imagined could be no way better expressed, than in manifesting your courtesies, and giving consent to your reasonable demands. For the first, I confesse (with thankes to the disposer of all things, and a true gratefull heart towardes you,) so many were the unexpected visitations, and unhoped kindnesses received, both from some among you, of my Acquaintance, and many other unknowne Well-willers of my Cause, that I was persweded to entertaine a much better conceit of Time, then I lately conceived, and assured my selfe that Vertue *had farre more followers than I supposed.*

Somewhat it disturbed me to behold our agees Favourites, whilst they frowned on my honest enterprises, to take unto their protection the egregiousts fopperies: yet much more was my contentment, in that I was respected by so many of You; *amongst whom there are some, who can and may as much dis-esteeme these, as they neglect mee: nor could I feare their Malice or Contempt, whilst I enjoyed your favours, who (howsoever you are under-valued by Fooles for a time) shall leave unto your posteritie so noble a memorie, that your names shall be reverenced by Kings, when many of these who now flourish with a shew of usurped* Greatnesse, *shall either weare out of beeing, or, dispoyled of all their patched Reputation, grow contemptible in the eyes of their beloved Mistrisse the* World. *Your* Love *it is that (enabling mee with patience to endure what is already past) hath made mee (also) carefull better to prepare my selfe for all future misadventures, by bringing to my consideration, what the passion of my just discontentments, had almost quite banished from my remembrance.*

Further, to declare my thankfulnesse, in making apparent my willing minde to be commanded in any services of love, which you shall thinke fitte (though I want abilitie to performe great matters) yet I have according to some of your requestes been contented to give way to the printing of these Eglogues, *which though it to many seeme a sleight matter, yet being well considered of, may prove a strong argument of my readinesse to give you content in a greater matter: for they being (as you well know) begotten with little care, and preserved with lesse respect, gave sufficient evidence that I meant (rather then any way to deceive your trust) to give the world occasion of calling my discretion in question, as I now assure my selfe This will: and the sooner, because such expectations (I perceive) there are (of I know not what Inventions) as would have been frustrated, though I had employed the utmost and very best of my endevours.*

Notwithstanding, for your sakes, I have here adventured once againe to make tryall of the worlds censures: and what hath received beeing, *from your* Loves, *I heere, rededicated to your* Worths, *which if your noble dispositions will like well of: or if you will but reasonably respect what yourselves drew mee unto, I shall be nothing displeased at others cavils, but resting my selfe contented with your good opinions, scorne all the rabble of uncharitable detractors. For none I know, will maligne it, except those, who either particularly malice my person, or professe themselves enemies to my former Bookes; who (saving those that were incensed on others speaches) as divers of you according to your protestations have observed, are either open enemies of our Church; men notoriously guilty of some particular abuses therein taxt, such malicious Critikes who have the repute of being judicious, by detracting from others; or at best such Guls, as never approve any thinge good, or learned, but either that which their shallow apprehensions can apply to the soothing of their owne opinions, or what, indeed rather, they understand not.*

Trust me, how ill soever it hath been rewarded, my love to my Country is inviolate: my thankefulnesse to you unfayned, my endevour to do everie man good; all my ayme content with honestie and this my paines (if it may be so tearmed) more to avoyde idlenesse, then for affectation of prayse: and if notwithstanding all this, I must yet, not onely rest my selfe content that my innocencie hath escaped with strict imprisonment (to the impayring of my state, and hinderance of my fortunes) but also be constrained to see my guiltlesse lines, suffer the despight of ill tongues: yet for my further encouragement, let me intreate the continuance of your first respect, wherein I shall finde that comfort as will be sufficient to make mee set light, and so much contemne all the malice of my adversaries, that ready to burst with the venome of their owne hearts, they shall see

My Minde enamoured on faire Vertues light,
Ascends the limits of their bleared sight,
And plac'd above their *Envy* doth contemne,
Nay, sit and laugh at their disdaine and them.

But, Noble Friends, *I make question neyther of yours, nor any honest mans respect, and therefore will no further urge it, nor trouble your patience: onely this Ile say, that you may not thinke me too well conceited of my selfe; though the* Time *were to blame in ill requiting my honest endeavours, which in the eyes of the world deserved better, yet somewhat I am assured there was in mee worthy that punishment, which when God shal give mee grace to see and amend, I doubt not but to finde that regard as will be fitting for so much merit as my labours may justly challenge. Meanwhile, the better to hold myself in esteeme with you, and amende the worlds opinion of* Vertue, *I will study to amende my selfe, that I may be yet more worthy to be called*

Your Friend,
Geo. Wyther.

William Cecil (Lord Burleigh), *Certain Precepts*, 1616.

The Induction.

BELOVED Sonne, the many religious and mortall vertues inherent in your matchless mother, under the wings of whose prudent and Godly government, your Infancy hath bene trayned and guyded up, together with your Education, under so zealous and Learned a Tutor, put mee rather in assurance then hope (as *Tullie* sometime expected from his Sonne, from the only hearing of *Cratippus* his Maister) that you are not ignorant of that summary bond, wherin you stand obliged to your Creator and Redeemer, which is onely able to make you happie, both heere and heereafter, in life and death. In mentioning whereof, I meane not onely a bare and Hystoricall knowledge, but with a reall and practical use adjoyned, without which, though with a seemly assumption, you could expresse to the World in a formall habite and living portrayture, all *Aristotles* Morall vertues, and walke that whole booke in *Life* and *Action:* yet are you but a vain and wretched Creature, the fayrest out-side of the miserablest inside, that ever was concealed by Toombe, or shadowing: and although I nothing doubt, your youth being guided, and your green vessell seasoned by such wholesome documents and instructions, derived from so all-sufficient Teachers, that you are not unfurnished of such needful helps, as may be furtherers to your life & conversation: yet that I may the better retaine and expresse the zealous affection, beseeming a Father to his Sonne, or that you should be forced to derive your stay and advice, rather from the rule of strangers, then from him from whom you are produced, and brought foorth.

Out of these foregoing considerations therefore, thinking it not unmeete, I have essayed from the affection of a Father, to give you such good advertisements and rules for the fitting and squaring of your life, as are gayned rather by my long experience and observation, then by much reading or Studie, beeing such (in my hope) with that good assistance, that shall *season your Youth like the deawe of Age;* to the ende, that you entring into this exorbitant and intangling World, may be the better furnished to avoyde those harmefull courses; whereinto these dangerous times, and your inexperience may easily insnare you. And because I would not confound your memorie, I have reduced them into tenne Precepts, which if next to *Moses* Tables, you imprint in your minde, you shall reape the benefite, and I the ende of my expectation and content. And thus they followe.

John Smith, *A Description of New England*, 1616.

TO THE HIGH HOPEFUL CHARLES,

Prince of Great Britaine.

SIR: So favourable was your most renowned and memorable Brother, Prince *Henry,* to all generous designes; that in my discovery of *Virginia,* I presumed to call two namelesse Headlands after my Soveraignes heires, *Cape Henry,* and *Cape Charles.* Since then, it beeing my chance to range some other parts of *America,* whereof I heere present your Highness the description in a Map; my humble sute is, you would please to change their Barbarous names, for such *English,* as Posterity may say, Prince *Charles* was their God-father. What here in this relation I promise my Countrey, let mee live or die the slave of scorne & infamy, if (having meanes) I make it not apparent; please God to blesse me but from such accidents as are beyond my power and reason to prevent. For my labours, I desire but such conditions as were promised me out of the gaines; and that your Highnesse would daigne to grace this Work, by your Princely and favourable respect unto it, and know mee to be

Your Highnesse true
and faithfull servant,
John Smith.

Thomas Campion, *The Third and Fourth Booke of Ayres,* 1617.

To the READER.

THE Apothecaries have Bookes of Gold, whose leaves being opened are so light as that they are subject to be shaken with the least breath, yet rightly handled, they serve both for ornament and use; such are light *Ayres.* But if any squeamish stomackes shall checke at two or three vaine Ditties in the end of this Booke, let them powre off the clearest and leave those as dregs in the bottome. Howsoever, if they be but conferred with the *Canterbury Tales* of that venerable Poet *Chaucer,* they will then appeare toothsome enough. Some words are in these Bookes which have beene cloathed in Musicke by others, and I am content they then served their turne: yet give mee now leave to make use of mine owne. Likewise you may finde here some three or foure Songs that have beene published before, but for them, I referre you to the Players Bill that is stiled, *Newly revived, with Additions,* for you shall finde all of them reformed, eyther in Words or Notes. To be briefe, all these Songs are mine if you expresse them well, otherwise they are your owne. Farewell.

Yours, as you are his,
THOMAS CAMPIAN.

Samuel Daniel, *Historie of England*, 1617.

TO THE MAJESTY OF ANNE OF DENMARKE, QUEENE OF ENGLAND,

Scotland, France and Ireland.

QUEENES, the Mothers of our Kings, by whom is continued the blessing of succession that preserves the Kingdome, having their parts running in the times wherein they live, are likewise interressed in the Histories thereof, which containe their memories and all that is left of them, when they have left to be in this world. And therefore to you, great Queene of *England* (and the greater by your love to the nation, and the blessing you have brought forth for the continuation of the future good thereof) doe I your humblest servant addresse this peece of our History; which, as it is a worke of mine, appertaines of right to your Majestie, being for the most parte done under your Roofe, during my attendance upon your sacred person: and if ever it shall come to bee an intire worke, and merit any acceptation in the world, it must remaine among the memorials of you, and your time, as brought forth under the splendor of your goodnes. Howsoever, this which is done shall yet shew how desirous I have beene to lay out my time and industry, as farre as my ability would extend to doe your Majestie, and my Country service in this kinde.

And though at high Altares, none but high Priests ought to sacrifize, yet vouchsafe mighty Queene, to accept this poore oblation from the hand of your Majesties

Humblest servant

Samuel Danyel.

Fynes Moryson, *An Itinerary*, 1617.

To the Right Honourable,

WILLIAM, *EARLE OF* PEMBROKE,

Lord Chamberlaine of his Majesties Household, *one of his Majesties most Honourable Privie* Counsell, and Knight of the most noble Order of the GARTER, &c.

Right Honourable,

SINCE *I had the happinesse imputed to* Salomons *Servants by the Queene of* Sheba *to stand sometimes before You, an eye and eare witnes of your Noble conversation with the worthy* Earle of Devonshire, (*my deceased Lord and Master*) *I ever admired your vertues and much honoured your Person. And because it is a thing no lesse commendable, gladly to receive favours from men of eminent worth, then with like choice to tender respect and service to them, I being now led by powerfull custome to seeke a Patron for this my Worke, and knowing that the weakest frames need strongest supporters, have taken the boldnes most humbly to commend it to your Honours protection: which vouchsafed, it shall triumph under the safegard of that massy shield; and my selfe shall not only acknowledge this high favour with humblest thankefulnesse, but with joy imbrace this occasion to avow my selfe now by publike profession,* (*as I have long been in private affection,*)

Your Honours most humble
and faithfull servant,
FYNES MORYSON.

Fynes Moryson, *An Itinerary,* 1617.

To the Reader.

FOR the First Part of this Worke, it containes only a briefe narration of daily journies with the rates of Coaches or Horses hired, the expences for horses and mans meat, the soyle of the Country, the situation of Townes and the descriptions thereof, together with all things there worthy to be seene: which Treatise in some obscure places is barren and unpleasant (espetially in the first beginning of the worke,) but in other places I hope you will judge it more pleasant, and in some delightfull, inducing you favorably to dispence with the barrennes of the former, inserted only for the use of unexperienced Travellers passing those waies. Againe, you may perhaps judge the writing of my daily expences in my journies to be needles & unprofitable, in respect of the continuall change of prices and rates in all Kingdoms: but they can never be more subject to change then the affaires of Martiall and civill Policie: in both which, the oldest Histories serve us at this day to good use. Thirdly and lastly, touching the First Part of this Worke, when you read my expences in unknowne Coynes, you may justly require the explaning of this obscurity, by expression of the values in the English Coynes. But I pray you to consider, that the adding of these severall values in each daies journy, had been an Herculean labour; for avoiding whereof, I have first set before the First Part, a briefe

Table expressing the value of the small Coynes most commonly spent, and also have expresly & particularly for each Dominion and most part of the Provinces, set downe at large, how these values answer the English Coynes, in a Chapter written of purpose to satisfie the most curious in this point, namely the fifth Chapter of the third Booke, being the last of this First Part: in which Chapter also I have briefly discoursed of the best means to exchange monies into forraigne parts.

Touching the Worke in generall, I wil truly say, that I wrote it swiftly, and yet slowly. This may seeme a strange Riddle, and not to racke your wit with the interpretation, my selfe will expound it: I wrote it swiftly, in that my pen was ready and nothing curious, as may appeare by the matter and stile: and I wrote it slowly, in respect of the long time past since I viewed these Dominions, and since I tooke this worke in hand. So as the Worke may not unfitly bee compared to a nose-gay of flowers, hastily snatched in many gardens, and with much leasure, yet carelesly and negligently bound together. The snatching is excused by the haste, necessary to Travellers, desiring to see much in short time. And the negligent binding, in true judgement needs no excuse, affected curiositie in poore subjects, being like rich imbroidery laid upon a frize jerken; so as in this case, onely the trifling away of much time, may bee imputed to my ignorance, dulnes or negligence, if my just excuse be not heard: in the rendering whereof I must crave your patience. During the life of the worthy *Earle of Devonshire,* my deceased Lord, I had little or no time to bestow in this kind. After his deth, I lost fully three yeers labor (in which I abstracted the Histories of these 12 Dominions thorow which I passed, with purpose to joyne them to the Discourses of the severall Commonwealths, for illustration and ornament; but when the worke was done, and I found the bulke thereof to swel, then I chose rather to suppresse them, then to make my gate bigger then my Citie.) And for the rest of the yeers, I wrote at leasure, giving (like a free and unhired workeman) much time to pleasure, to necessary affaires, and to divers and long distractions. If you consider this, and withall remember, that the worke is first written in Latine, then translated into English, and that in divers Copies, no man being able by the first Copie to put so large a worke in good fashion. And if you will please also to take knowledge from me, that to save expences, I wrote the greatest part with my owne hand, and almost all the rest with the slowe pen of my servant: then I hope the losse of time shall not be imputed unto me. Againe, for the worke in generall, I professe not to write it to any curious wits, who can indure nothing but extractions and quintessences: nor yet to great Statesmen, of whose reading I confesse it is unworthy: but only unto the unexperienced, who shall desire to view forraign kingdomes. And these may, the rather by this direction, make better use of what they see, heare, and reade, then my selfe did. If active men never reade it, I shall wish them no lesse good successe in their affaires. If contemplative men shall reade it at leasure, making choice of the subjects fitting their humours, by the Table of the Contents, and casting away the booke when they are weary of reading, perhaps they may finde some delight: onely in case of distaste, I pray them remember, to and for whom it was written. To conclude, if you be as well affected to me, as I am to you, howsoever I deserve no thanks, no doubt I shall be free from blame. And so I wish you all happinesse, remaining

Yours in due respect,

Fynes Moryson.

J. C., *The Two Merry Milke-Maids*, 1620.

THE PRINTER TO THE READER.

EVERY *Writer must governe his Penne according to the Capacitie of the Stage he writes too, both in the Actor and the Auditor. This had the happinesse to please, as it was meant, the greater part and of them not the worst. If there be discoverie made of the Conjuring Words, you'le find the Witchcraft: no true Spirit will be stir'd with 'hem; haply, a malicious. It was made more for the Eye, then the Eare; lesse for the Hand, then eyther: and had not false Copies travail'd abroad (even to surbating) this had kept in; for so farre the Author was from seeking fame in the publishing, that hee could have wisht it bound about with the Ring. Some good words here you shall finde for your Money, else it keepes not touch with the Title. Receive it well, and though in this he give you no ill, yet hereafter he hath promis'd you better Language.*

William Loe, *A Months Minde,* 1620.

To his much respected good frend Mr. THOMAS BARKER one of the assistants of the worthy companie of the Marchants Adventurers, residing at Hamborough.

The blessing of both worlds in Christ Jesus.

W*ELBELOVED. There is nothing more comfortable to a spirituall minded man then to muse & meditate of his departure hence into the blessed sight of Christ in the other life. Yet to a wordling that would build up a rest for his body here, & sing a requiem to his soule in this vale of teares, nothing is more fearefull & hiddeous then for him to heare death spoken of. We must therefore examine our selves, whether we can sing a song of Sion in this exile and banishment, whether we can solace our selves, in hymnes & songs, of our ends and departure hence. For we must hence: nothing more sure; but the tyme when, the place where, & the manner how: nothing more unsure. It is sufficient that God telleth us our life is but a flower that fadeth, an hower that passeth, a shadowe that departeth, a vanity that vexeth, a moment that warneth, a nothing when we* *have done all we can. For our thoughts, our faults, our purposes, our projects, our loves, our lives, when our breath departeth, perisheth in the twinckling of an eie. O then let us meditate & muse to our selves, and sing, & say to our soules that our end & the last things are not the least but the best things that we can consider of to mortifie us, & make us meete for the saving mercies of god in Christ; to which I recomend you in my dearest love, & rest.*

Yours in life, & death,
W. Loe.

George Sandys, *Ovid's Metamorphosis*, 1621–26.

To the most High and Mightie Prince CHARLES, King of *Great Britaine, France, and* IRELAND

SIR,

Y*OUR Gracious acceptance of the first fruites of my Travels, when You were our Hope, as now our Happinesse; hath actuated both Will and Power to the finishing of this Peece: being limn'd by that unperfect light which was snatcht from the howers of night and repose. For the day was not mine, but dedicated to the service of your Great Father, and your Selfe: which, had it proved as fortunate as faithfull, in me, and others more worthy; we had hoped, ere many yeares had turned about, to have presented You with a rich and wel-peopled Kingdome; from whence now, with my selfe, I onely bring this Composure:*

Inter victrices Hederam tibi serpere Laurus.

It needeth more then a single denization, being a double Stranger. Sprung from the Stocke of the ancient Romanes; but bred in the New-world, of the rudenesse whereof it cannot but participate; especially having Warres and Tumults to bring it to light in stead of the Muses. But how ever unperfect, Your favour is able to sup-

ply; and to make it worthy of life, if you judge it not unworthy of your Royall Patronage. Long may you live to be, as you are, the Delight and Glorie of your People: and slowly, yet surely, exchange your mortal Diadem for an immortall. So wishes

Your Majesties
most humble
Servant
George Sandys.

Beaumont and Fletcher, *Philaster,* 1622.

To the Reader.

COURTEOUS Reader. *Philaster* and *Arethusa,* his love, have laine so long a bleeding, by reason of some dangerous and gaping wounds which they received in the first Impression, that it is wondered how they could goe abroad so long, or travaile so farre as they have done. Although they were hurt neither by me, nor the Printer; yet I knowing and finding by experience how many well-wishers they have abroad, have adventured to bind up their wounds & to enable them to visite upon better tearmes such friends of theirs as were pleased to take knowledge of them so mained and deformed as they at the first were; and if they were then gracious in your sight, assuredly they will now finde double favour being reformed, and set forth suteable to their birth and breeding.

By your serviceable Friend,
Thomas Walkley.

Patrick Hannay, *Sheretine and Mariana*, 1622.

TO THE TRULIE HONOURABLE AND NOBLE LADY LUCIE COUNTESS OF Bedford.

IT is a continued custome (Right honourable) that what passeth the Presse, is Dedicated to some one of eminent quality: Worth of the personage to whom, or a private respect of the partie by whom it is offered, being chiefe causes thereof, the one for protection and honour, the other for a thankfull remembrance. Moved by both these, I present this small Poem (now exposed to publike censure) to your Honour: first knowing the foreplacing of your Name (for true worth so deservedly well knowne to the world) will not only be a defence against malignant carpers, but also an addition of grace. Secondly, the obligation of gratitude (whereby I am bound to your Ladyships service) which cannot be cancelled, shall be hereby humbly acknowledged. If it please (that being the end of these endevours) I have my desire. Daine to accept thereof (Madam) with a favourable aspect, whereby I shall be incouraged, and more strictly tyed to remaine

Ever your Honour's, in
all humble dutie,
Patrick Hannay.

Henry Peacham, *The Compleat Gentleman,* 1622.

To my Reader.

I *AM not ignorant (Judicious Reader) how many peeces of the most curious Masters have beene uttered to the world of this Subject, as* Plutarch, Erasmus, Vives, Sadolet, Sturmius, Osorius, *Sir* Thomas Eliot, *M.* Askham, *with sundry others; so that my small Taper among so many Torches, were as good out, as seeming to give no light at all. I confesse it true. But as rare and curious stamps upon Coynes, for their varietie and strangenesse, are daily enquired after, and bought up, though the Silver be all one and common with ours: so fares it with Bookes, which (as* Meddailes) *beare the Pictures and devices of our various Invention, though the matter be the same, yet for variety sake they shall bee read, yea (and as the same dishes drest after a new fashion) perhaps please the tastes of many better. But this regard neither mooved me. When I was beyond the Seas, and in a part of* France, *adjoyning upon* Artoise, *I was invited oftentimes to the house of a Noble personage, who was both a great Souldier and an excellent Scholler; and one day above the rest, as we sate in an open and goodly Gallerie at dinner, a young* English *Gentleman, who, desirous to travaile, had beene in* Italy *and many other places, fortuned to come to his house; and (not so well furnished for his returne home as was fitting) desired entertainement into his service. My Lord, who could speake as little* English, *as my*

Country-man French, *bad him welcome, and demaunded by me of him, what hee could doe: For I keepe none (quoth he) but such as are commended for some good qualitie or other, and I give them good allowance; some an hundred, some sixtie, some fiftie Crownes by the yeare: and calling some about him, (very Gentleman-like, as well in their behaviour, as apparell) This* (saith he) *rideth and breaketh my great Horses; this is an excellent Lutenist, this a good Painter and Surveyer of land, this a passing Linguist and Scholler, who instructeth my Sonnes, &c. Sir* (quoth this young man) *I am a Gentleman borne, and can onely attend you in your Chamber, or waite upon your Lordship abroad. See (quoth* Monsieur de Ligny, *for so was his name) how your Gentry of* England *are bred: that when they are distressed, or want means in a strange Countrey, they are brought up neither to any qualitie to preferre them, nor have they so much as the Latine tongue to helpe themselves withall. I knew it generally to be true, but for the time, and upon occasion excused it as I could; yet he was received, and after returned to his friends in good fashion. Hereby I onely give to know, that there is nothing more deplorable than the breeding in generall of our Gentlemen, none any more miserable then one of them, if he fall into miserie in a strange Country, which I can impute to no other thing, than the remisnesse of Parents, and negligence of Masters in their youth. Wherefore at my comming over, considering the great forwardnesse, and proficience of children in other Countries, the backwardnesse and rawnesse of ours; the industry of Masters there, the ignorance and idlenesse of most of ours; the exceeding care of Parents in their childrens Education, the negligence of ours: Being taken through change of ayre with a Quartane Fever, that leasure I had* ἀπὸ παροξυσμοῦ *as I may truly say, by fits I employed upon this Discourse for the private use of a Noble young Gentleman my friend, not intending it should ever see light, as you may perceive by the plaine and shallow current of the Discourse, fitted to a young and tender capacitie. Howsoever, I have done it, and if thou shalt find herein any thing that may content, at the least, not distaste thee, I shall be glad and encouraged to a more serious Peece: if neither, but out of a malignant humour, disdaine what I have done, I care not; I have pleased my selfe: and long since learned,* Envie, *together with her Sister* Ignorance, *to harbour only in the basest and most degenerate breast.*

William Shakespeare, *Comedies, Histories, & Tragedies*, 1623.

TO THE MOST NOBLE AND INCOMPARABLE PAIRE OF BRETHREN

WILLIAM

Earle of Pembroke, &c. Lord Chamberlaine to the

Kings most Excellent Majesty.

AND

PHILIP

Earle of Montgomery, &c. Gentleman of his Majesties Bed-Chamber. Both Knights of the most Noble Order of the Garter, and our singular good

LORDS.

Right Honourable,

W*HILST we studie to be thankful in our particular, for the many favors we have received from your L. L. we are falne upon the ill fortune, to mingle two the most diverse things that can bee, feare, and rashnesse; rashnesse in the enterprize, and feare of the successe. For, when we valew the places your H. H. sustaine, we cannot but know* *their dignity greater, then to descend to the reading of these trifles: and, while we name them trifles, we have depriv'd our selves of the defence of our Dedication. But since your L. L. have beene pleas'd to thinke these trifles some-thing heeretofore; and have prosequuted both them, and their Authour living, with so much favour: we hope, that (they out-living him, and he not having the fate, common with some, to be exequutor to his owne writings) you will use the like indulgence toward them, you have done unto their parent. There is a great difference, whether any Booke choose his Patrones, or finde them; this hath done both. For, so much were your L. L. likings of the severall parts, when they were acted, as before they were published, the Volume ask'd to be yours. We have but collected them, and done an office to the dead, to procure his Orphanes, Guardians; without ambition either of selfe-profit, or fame: onely to keepe the memory of so worthy a Friend, & Fellow alive, as was our* Shakespeare, *by humble offer of his playes, to your most noble patronage. Wherein, as we have justly observed, no man to come neere your L. L. but with a kind of religious addresse; it hath bin the height of our care, who are the Presenters, to make the present worthy of your H. H. by the perfection. But, there we must also crave our abilities to be considered, my Lords. We cannot go beyond our owne powers. Country hands reach foorth milke, creame, fruites, or what they have: and many Nations (we have heard) that had not gummes & incense, obtained their requests with a leavened Cake. It was no fault to approch their Gods, by what meanes they could: and the most, though meanest, of things are made more precious, when they are dedicated to Temples. In that name therefore, we most humbly consecrate to your H. H. these remaines of your servant* Shakespeare, *that what delight is in them, may be ever your L. L. the reputation his, & the faults ours, if any be committed, by a payre so carefull to shew their gratitude both to the living, and the dead, as is*

Your Lordshippes most bounden,
John Heminge.
Henry Condell.

William Shakespeare, *Comedies, Histories, & Tragedies,* 1623.

To the great Variety of Readers.

FROM the most able, to him that can but spell: There you are number'd. We had rather you were weighd. Especially, when the fate of all Bookes depends upon your capacities: and not of your heads alone, but of your purses. Well! It is now publique, & you wil stand for your priviledges wee know: to read, and censure. Do so, but buy it first. That doth best commend a Booke, the Stationer saies. Then, how odde soever your braines be, or your wisedomes, make your licence the same, and spare not. Judge your sixe-pen'orth, your shillings worth, your five shillings worth at a time; or higher, so you rise to the just rates, and welcome. But, what ever you do, Buy. Censure will not drive a Trade, or make the Jacke go. And though you be a Magistrate of wit, and sit on the Stage at *Black-Friers,* or the *Cock-pit,* to arraigne Playes dailie, know, these Playes have had their triall alreadie, and stood out all appeales; and do now come forth quitted rather by a Decree of Court, then any purchas'd Letters of commendation.

It had bene a thing, we confesse, worthie to have bene wished, that the Author himselfe had liv'd to have set forth, and overseen his owne writings. But since it hath bin ordain'd otherwise, and he by death departed from that right, we pray you do not envie his Friends, the office of their care, and paine, to have collected & publish'd them; and so to have publish'd them, as where (before) you were abus'd with diverse stolne, and surreptitious copies, maimed, and deformed by the frauds and stealthes of injurious impostors, that expos'd them: even those, are now offer'd to your view cur'd, and perfect of their limbes; and all the rest, absolute in their numbers, as he conceived them. Who, as he was a happie imitator of Nature, was a most gentle expresser of it. His mind and hand went together: and what he thought, he uttered with that easinesse, that wee have scarse received from him a blot in his papers. But it is not our province, who onely gather his works, and give them you, to praise him. It is yours that reade him. And there we hope, to your divers capacities, you will finde enough, both to draw, and hold you: for his wit can no more lie hid, then it could be lost. Reade him, therefore; and againe, and againe: and if then you doe not like him, surely you are in some manifest danger, not to understand him. And so we leave you to other of his Friends, whom if you need, can bee your guides: if you neede them not, you can leade your selves, and others. And such Readers we wish him.

John Heminge.
Henrie Condell.

NOTES

NOTES

Page 29. This famous book is conspicuous as the earliest anthology of verse in the language. Richard Tottel was evidently an enterprising man, as he also published Grafton's *Chronicles of England,* Painter's *Palace of Pleasure,* and North's *Dial of Princes* in addition to notable law books. Except for Grimald who appears to have been the editor at least of the first edition, the collection is made of verse of the previous generation. The emulation to do as well in English as the ancients is a characteristic note of the moment.

Page 30. John Stow, famous chronicler of London, was likewise a writer of the most popular compendious histories of his age. This *Summary,* especially, went through ten editions between 1565 and 1604. It is a commentary on the nature of authorship in his time that despite his extraordinary industry and the large sales of his books, his was a lifetime struggle with poverty.

Page 32. Ascham was tutor to the royal children of Henry VIII. Besides *Toxophilus,* a defense of archery, he left behind him a treatise in education which he called *The Scholemaster.* In publishing his work, his widow offers a justification of the practice of dedication and touches upon the duties alike of the author and the patron.

Page 34. *Gorboduc,* the earliest tragedy in English, was the first of a long series of similar plays written and acted by the amateur gentlemen of the Inns of Court. In this case Elizabeth herself was present; and there is little doubt but that these young authors were fully conscious of the parallel between King Gorboduc's unwisdom in dividing his kingdom and the unprotected, unmarried state of their Queen. Productions of this kind were private in their nature, and it was abhorrent to the gentility of the authors to contemplate publication; hence the explanation of the address.

Page 36. This address is one of the earlier examples of what we cannot but call intentional mystification. It being against the gentility of any well-born man to descend to the degradation of print, and the itch to so appear being none the less strong upon him, it became necessary to justify publication. Into the intricacies of these labyrinths it is needless to inquire. Gascoigne's book was a collection, and the better opinion seems to be that even the lyrics of the volume are his.

Page 39. This second anthology of verse is supposed to have been edited by Richard Edwards.

Page 41. This charming little prayer is a fitting preface to the memoirs of a personage of state and importance in the courts of both Elizabeth and James.

Page 42. The earlier days of Elizabeth were full of discovery not only geographical but also literary. Among such were the many tales and stories of Italian fiction wrought by these English translators into prose, verse, or drama. This dedication is interesting because of its criticism of current action on the stage. The story in question was later utilized by Shakespeare in *Measure for Measure.*

Page 45. Gosson was a Puritan objector to everything which he happened personally to disapprove; wherefore his attack upon the stage which was rendered the more violent in that he was a renegade playwright himself. Gosson dedicated his *School of Abuse* to Sir Philip Sidney without obtaining permission, whether in satire or in sober earnest cannot now be determined.

Page 50. This address offers an example of Lyly's euphuistic diction which strove for grace, smoothness, and appeasable ornament. Our modern feeling towards such rhetorical efforts must change from a sense of its variety to an appreciation of its desire to better English speech and writing.

Page 52. This is a fitting dedication of a noble translation of a noble original, which must always interest in that it was the one source of Shakespeare in which, as has been well said, "he met his match."

Page 54. Richard Mulcaster, by some supposed to be ridiculed as Holofernes in *Loves Labours Lost,* was the first master of the Merchant Tailor's School; and among his pupils was Spenser. His *Positions* is an original and able plan for the education of the middle classes in which he emphasizes several features which we regard as quite modern: physical training, music, for example, and the education of women. Another aspect of a fruitful life represents Mulcaster as associated with the drama at court.

Page 58. This treatise seems to have been the immediate result of the young prince's study with his famous tutor Buchanan. It contrasts in its dogmatism and insistence in adherence to positive rules of technique with the slightly earlier treatise of Gascoigne's *Certayne Notes of Instruction.*

Page 61. William Warner was an attorney who turned to writing. According to Anthony-à-Wood, he was "more a friend to poetry, history, and romance than to logic and philosophy." His one important work, *Albions England,* was completed by accretions in nine editions between 1586 and 1612 and may be described as an episodic narrative in verse mingling legendary material with authentic history. Warner enjoyed an extraordinary popularity. The dedication displays a sweet natural modesty coupled with respect for the dignity of his work.

Page 63. The celebrated musician William Byrd is remembered aside from his art as the fortunate recipient of a monopoly to print and sell both English and foreign music. Byrd was a sometime organist of Lincoln Cathedral and a gentleman of the Chapel Royal. He was the founder of the English madrigal school. His *Psalmes, Sonnets, and Songs of Sadness and Piety* is the earliest volume containing English madrigals.

Page 65. As to the writings of Sir Philip Sidney, "England's paragon," it is always to be remembered that none of them was written to print. According to the fashion they circulated in manuscript. They were copied again and again into commonplace books by admirers; and it was only after Sidney's death that the *Arcadia,* containing most of his other writings with it, "escaped into print."

Page 67. Thomas Watson was a classical scholar of notable achievement, one of the early sonneteers, and the earliest of lyrists to write words for music. He is represented in several of the poetical miscellanies of his day. *Melibœus,* a Latin elegy in hexameters, occasioned by the death of his patron, Sir Francis Walsingham, is dedicated to the latter's cousin, Sir Thomas Walsingham. In 1587, an unauthorized English translation of Watson's Latin poem *Amyntas* won considerable fame for Fraunce. Therefore Watson published an English translation of *Melibœus* and dedicated it to his patron's daughter, Lady Francis, widow of Sir Philip Sidney. Spenser refers to Watson as both poet and patron of poets.

Page 68. This early report on the state of Russia begot a note of protest from the Eastland merchants who remonstrated with Burghley lest it give offense to the Russian court. In this history is now repeating itself.

Page 70. This note of the printer illustrates a very usual reason why certain plays came into print at certain times.

Page 71. It would be of great value could we more fully know the relation of such writers, procurers of copy, and general utility men about the publishers of books as Nashe appears to have been. This publication of *Astrophel and Stella* was purely a mercantile transaction; and the additions of this poetry "of sundry other noblemen and gentlemen," among them Samuel Daniel, was purely padding to increase the price of the book. Nashe was evidently endeavoring to earn his fee in this case.

Page 77. This dedication offers an excellent example of the attitude of a gentleman towards the products of his brain. It is to the credit of Wilmot that when he revised this tragedy, originally the work of several authors, he rewrote it, thus taking the entire responsibility.

Page 80. This famous autobiographical tract is popularly supposed to have been written to defray Greene's funeral expenses. The story of Roberto is unimportant; the epistle to "his quondam acquaintance" is notorious alike for its mention of Shakespeare, the earliest in print, and for its warning to his fellow playwrights against him.

Page 88. Although the address "To The Gentlemen Readers" of this pamphlet declares that Chettle was the editor of Greene's posthumous

Groatsworth of Wit, Chettle denies any responsibility for the offense in Greene's book offered to his colleagues in playwriting, and refers to Shakespeare as one whose "demeanor [is] no lesse civill than he excelent in the qualitie he professes." Henry Chettle was a popular dramatist and pamphleteer. *Kind-Hartes Dreame* assembles a group of personages who discuss with gusto and humor the vices and foibles of certain classes of his time.

Page 93. An avowed Romanist, Constable lived much abroad. His sonnets adhere more closely to the Italian form and spirit than was common among Elizabethan sonneteers. Published in 1592, the height of the "sonnet craze," Constable enjoyed a somewhat exaggerated reputation for his eloquence rather than his passion.

Page 94. Daniel was a tutor to noble folk and the earliest of the followers of Sidney in the sonnet. His work in this trend was first published at the end of Newman's unauthorized edition of *Astrophel and Stella.* In self-defense, Daniel himself issued most of these and thirty others to which he gave the title *Delia.*

Page 96. Barnes is the immediate follower of Sidney in the Italianate form, not only of his sonnets but also in his experimental practice of other varieties of Italian verse. The son of a bishop, Barnes was intimate with many great folk, as his dedicatory sonnets attest.

Page 97. Giles Fletcher, the elder, makes no secret of his method as a sonneteer, announcing on the title-page of *Licia* that his "poems of love" were written "to the imitation of the best Latin poets, and others." In his dedicatory address, he deprecates the notion that his book is based on personal experience. In his epistle to the reader he laughingly challenges his critics to identify his lady-love, Licia, with any living woman.

Page 100. In the preface to this pious production, Nashe made amends to Gabriel Harvey, whose fame and reputation he so rashly assailed in defending his friend Robert Greene. But in his *New Letter of Notable Contents,* Harvey scornfully rejected this apology, which was offered in all sincerity. Nashe therefore recalled, as far as was in his power, the copies to which his amends were prefixed, and, reprinting the title-page with the date 1594, added a long epistle "to the reader" in which he treated Harvey with the asperity which he had courted.

Page 102. In this beautiful but frankly sensual narrative poem, Shakespeare was following a contemporary fashion illustrated in Lodge's earlier *Glaucus and Scilla,* Marlowe's *Hero and Leander,* and many later examples. Interest attaches to the statement that this was the "first heir" of Shakespeare's invention. The poem enjoyed great popularity, seven editions appearing before the close of Elizabeth's reign.

Page 103. Churchyard's *Pleasant Conceite* is a pleasing example of the many poetical quips and small devices which were employed to amuse and beguile the Queen in the intimacy of her court. This particular effort was written in gratitude for a pension granted to Churchyard by the Queen, and forms part of an entertainment presented to Her Majesty at Hampton Court on New Year's Day, 1593–94.

Page 104. This is Kyd's contribution to the group of plays known as French Seneca in English. A translation, in this case of Garnier, like several of its class, it is doubtful if it was intended for the stage. Kyd's promise of a second play of the type, *Portia,* remained unfulfilled.

Page 106. William Percy was a son of the Earl of Northumberland and a friend of Barnabe Barnes. In twenty *Sonnets to the Fairest Coelia,* he plaintively and vainly begs his mistress's favor after the accepted manner of such "toys and amorous devices."

Page 107. Shakespeare's only other dedicatory letter is this prefixed to *The Rape of Lucrece.* It has been thought to express progress in intimacy with his patron and to record the promise of "some graver labour." This bitter and tragic story enjoyed a popularity almost equal to *Venus and Adonis,* for eight editions were called for between 1594 and 1611.

Page 108. In *Cynthia,* a poem based on classical allegory and reminiscent of Peele's *Arraignment of Paris,* 1584, the golden apple is awarded to Queen Elizabeth. Twenty sonnets and an ode in easy trochaics are appended, as well as a languid tragedy, *Cassandra.* Barnfield wrote lyrically so well that some of his poems found their way into the *Passionate Pilgrim,* 1599, a collection attributed to Shakespeare.

Page 111. Francis Sabbie appears as a schoolmaster at Lichfield in 1587 and as the author also of several versifications of scripture. *Pan's Pipe* conforms to the contemporary mode of the pastoral popularized by Spenser and to the passing effort to write English hexameters in emulation of classical examples.

Page 112. Henry Olney, ignorant of Ponsonby's entry of Sidney's *Defence of Poesie* in the Stationers' Register, proceeded to publish the treatise; and to this he prefixed the appreciative and explanatory epistle "To the Reader." As a result, two editions of Sidney's famous essay written *c.* 1583 appeared in 1595. The *Apologie for Poetry,* the earliest noteworthy piece of English criticism, was apparently written in reply to Gosson's attack on plays and poetry and to the latter's presumptuous dedication.

Page 113. Robert Southwell, a Jesuit priest interested in recovering the nation to Catholicism, was detected, confined in prison two and a half years, and finally hanged. While in prison, he wrote most of his poems. The sincerity, deep conviction, fervor, and piety of the man are reflected in all he wrote. *St. Peter's Complaint,* a long religious poem, is really a succession of separate studies on the remorseful fall of St. Peter. It is remarkable for the great number and ingenuity of the conceits. Southwell's object was to rescue the art of poetry from the worldly uses to which it had been almost solely devoted.

Page 115. In August, 1591, Lodge sailed with Cavendish, the circumnavigator, for South America. To judge by the mere accident of geography, the earliest specimen of "American literature" is Lodge's pertinently titled *A Margarite of America,* written, according to the prefatory matter, in the Strait of Magellan four years prior to publication and under circumstances most hazardous. The story was taken from a Spanish work in the Jesuit library at Santos, Brazil. Lodge, student and soldier, wrote drama, romance, lyrical poetry, verse satire, pamphlets, and translations besides maintaining the practice and reputation of one of the foremost physicians of London.

Page 119. An immortal dedication to an immortal book. In it we have illustrated alike the elaborate courtesy and the fine independence of the Elizabethan spirit.

Page 120. In dedicating the first edition of his essays, only ten in number, to his brother, Francis Bacon asserted that he published them because an unauthorized edition was about to be printed. To call on the aid of the officers of state or the master of the Stationers' Company to prevent a few essays escaping into print might suggest that he attached too much importance to them; or, again, that they contained something which he did not desire to be made public. As the question of publication was raised, he proceeded to take the sensible course and sent them to the press himself; despite his theory that his works should appear only posthumously.

Page 122. Nicholas Breton was apparently inducted into authorship by his stepfather, the poet Gascoigne; and he came to share with so many of the writers of his time the generous patronage of Mary Sidney, "Sidney's sister, Pembroke's mother." Entirely English in style and sentiment, and with inimitable charm and humor, Breton has given us a vivid picture of the domestic life of the Elizabethan. In prose he excels in dialogues and character studies which range from the laborer to the courtier. In *The Scholler and the Souldiour,* a dialogue, one defends learning, the other martial discipline.

Page 123. Dowland, the most famous lutanist of his day, carried the repute of English music to the continent and was lutanist to the King of Denmark and otherwise patronized by the great in his travels from place to place. In a famous sonnet by Barnfield, attributed by error to Shakespeare, Dowland is placed in music on a par with Spenser in poetry.

Page 128. This dedication of the earliest pamphlet of a man who was later to become distinguished as an able dramatist is here included as a graceful and poetic bid for patronage.

Page 130. Deloney wrote the best-sellers in what might be called the literature of the middle classes, the tradesmen and such of the other workmen as were literate enough to read his stories of the shoemakers, cloth traders, men of their own kind. Such works of his as *The Gentle Craft, Thomas of*

Reading, and *Jack of Newbury* enjoyed so great a popularity that the story of the first, at least, passed into the form of a penny chapbook.

Page 131. Marlowe, the great tragic writer, left behind him, after his tragic death at Deptford in 1593, an unfinished narrative poem of exquisite beauty in the contemporary fashion of *Venus and Adonis.* While really a paraphrase of Musæus, Marlowe made of his poem a new work; and Chapman, who appears to have been his personal friend, completed it with a skill in which he outdid his former efforts. *Hero and Leander* continued long popular.

Page 133. *The Scourge of Villainy* is one of three celebrated satires in decasyllables written towards the end of Elizabeth's reign in emulation and imitation of the verse satire of Horace and Juvenal. Marston wrote *The Scourge* under the pseudonym W. Kinsayder, and enjoyed with his fellows Donne and Hall the popularity of a contemporary scandal. His book was ordered burned by the common hangman in 1599. A notorious and supererogatory address to Everlasting Oblivion concludes Marston's work.

Page 135. In a prefatory sonnet by A. M., Bodenham is addressed as

> Arts lover, Learnings friend,
> First causer and collector of these floures.

Belvedere is a compilation of poetical extracts made up of single lines and couplets arranged under various captions, such as God, Heaven, Conscience, Religion, and Truth. The authors' names are not annexed to the extracts, but the poets to whom Bodenham admits his obligations, not excluding Spenser and Shakespeare, are mentioned in the preface. Bodenham was the editor of the collection.

Page 139. *England's Helicon,* the most delightful of early poetical anthologies, was apparently projected by Bodenham, to whom A. B. doubtless refers as "her rightful Patrone." The actual editor may have been A. B. or more probably Nicholas Ling, well-known publisher. Whoever selected the poems showed wide reading and good taste. In his preface to the reader, Ling endeavored to assuage any author who objected to appearing in print or any stationer who felt he had been robbed.

Page 142. This admirable play, possibly acted as early as 1597, is one of the earliest, as it remained one of the most successful, comedies specifically of London life. A notice of a royal performance is made in the dedication. This dedicatory epistle is unusual in setting forth the argument of the play.

Page 143. William Kemp, a fellow of Shakespeare's, comic actor and dancer, successor to Richard Tarlton, gained popularity through his jigs at the close of plays. In 1599, Kemp undertook the morris dance from London to Norwich. His journey required twenty-three days, but he spent only nineteen days in actual dancing. The Mayor of Norwich arranged a triumphal entry for him. And in 1600, he published an account of this journey as *Kemp's Nine Days' Wonder,* which incidentally presents a rough picture of English manners. There are innumerable contemporary allusions to this notorious "dance."

Page 145. The brief epistle to the reader and the poem itself, based on the theme of gratitude, together form a whole. The appreciative disposition of Elizabethan authors depending upon patronage is reflected in this little piece of work. Breton dedicated it to Mistris Mary Gate in an acrostic and prose epistle. The poem is didactic, but Breton's piety is not of the clamorous or demonstrative kind. Brightness, tenderness, freshness, and purity describe him.

Page 146. In his *Observations in the Art of English Poesy,* we meet with Campion as a critic of existing English verse, and, strange in such a master of this art, the advocate of classical prosody in English. This pamphlet and Daniel's answer, *The Defense of Ryme,* were the last two guns in a long and fruitless controversy.

Page 148. Davison was alike a collector and a poet. This is the last of the Elizabethan anthologies of lyrics. Davison's literary instructions are not uninteresting.

Page 151. Alexander, later created Earl of Stirling by King James, was one of the horde of Scottish gentlemen that accompanied that monarch on his assumption of the crown of England. Like his friend Drummond, Stirling was a follower of Sidney and of the contemporary French lyric. The sonnets, *Aurora,* appeared in 1604, but doubtless belong in point of composition to the sonnet decade 1590–1600.

Page 152. This preface sheds an interesting light on the relation of the dramatist to the printers of the day; though perhaps Marston's protestations as to this, as to his innocence with respect to satirical allusions, are to be taken with a grain of salt.

Page 154. Of Scoloker practically nothing is known. This epistle, in a fashion becoming prevalent after 1600, satirizes the address to the reader, the search for a patron, and burlesques the attack on the unhappy printer for all the shortcomings of the book. The epistle is otherwise interesting for its allusions to Sidney's *Arcadia,* to "friendly Shakespeare" and his plays, *Hamlet* in particular.

Page 157. It was this celebrated tract that justified Bacon's proud boast that he took "all learning for his province." In his *Advancement* the author clears the ground, maps out his great purpose, and lays the foundation of that stupendous *Instauratio Magna* which he was destined to leave a noble but hopelessly uncompleted structure.

Page 161. Jonson was always a theorist and never happier than when defending or explaining something to the inferior understandings of other men.

Page 163. Thomas Dekker wrote plays, civic pageants, lyrics, and a voluminous number of pamphlets. He is one of the earliest representatives of a new type, the professional writer. His humanity and direct realism entitle him to an important place among those who have faithfully portrayed London street life. The dedication of this pamphlet dares the selection of a patron personally unacquainted with the author. The theme reverts to the mediaeval vision in which a trial is conducted of those who, once familiar figures of the streets of London, are now tried for their sins.

Page 165. These *Poemes, Lyrick and Pastorall,* contain some of Drayton's choicest work. His odes are the earliest in the English language and some of them are the best. Notable is the famous *Ballad of Agincourt,* the most spirited of English martial lyrics, and the superb ode, *To the Virginian*

Voyage. The preface to the volume affords a brief discussion of the ode. Drayton's reputation for probity as a man equaled his fame as a poet.

Page 167. This address is clearly a satire on Jonson's mode of work and belongs to the moment when the two satirists happened to be at enmity. There were other moments when they were the dearest of friends.

Page 168. Day was described by Jonson as a "rogue"; but he was likewise a poet of rare quality and an excellent playwright. The independence of the tone of this address towards the critics seems more than a pose.

Page 169. Heywood's words in this often-quoted passage offer an explanation of conditions between publishers and playwrights which is illuminating in the midst of much darkness.

Page 170. This bit of evidence as to what was regarded in its age as timely publication is of the utmost value. It seems an over-refinement of criticism to assume that Middleton's words apply only to dramas of a satirical type. Clearly, the sale of any book must depend on such repute as it may be able to acquire.

Page 171. This tract, ascribed to Sir Walter Raleigh, urges an expedition to Virginia, chiefly on religious grounds: to spread Christianity among the savages, as a measure to relieve Great Britain of surplus population, and for personal advantages by way of prospective wealth and happiness. Views of worldly policy and religious duty are judiciously blended. The final sentence of the pamphlet tells us the author is unable to assist in the desired adventure either in purse or in person.

Page 173. Richard Hakluyt, geographer, lecturer on cosmography, and clergyman, author of *The Principal Navigations, Voyages and Discoveries of the English Nation,* 1589, translated *Virginia Richly Valued,* "written by a Portugall gentleman of Elvas," 1557, and published it in 1609 probably under the patronage of the Virginia Company. This work contains the best extant account of Don Ferdinando de Soto's expedition and affords us one of the most fascinating and curious accounts relative to the history of Florida.

Page 179. Into the difficulties attending the explanation of this preface it is not necessary to enter. Our interest must center in this avowal of contemporary opinion, the gird at "the grand possessors," and the extraordinary prophecy as to the Shakespeare quartos when "out of sale."

Page 181. Campion was not only a musician and a poet, but a theorist, both of poetry and the kindred art, as this learned work, *A New Way of Making Fowre parts in Counter-point,* discloses. This particular work deservedly remained for many years the standard textbook and the musical student's compendium on the subject.

Page 188. Fletcher's address is of interest for its definition of the pastoral drama and for the reasons which he assigns for the failure of this particular play.

Page 190. Robert Jones was another notable musician in his day, as appears from his several collections dedicated to personages of rank. Unlike Campion, Jones appears to have been more the collector at least as far as the words of his songs are concerned, and in consequence these collections are often unequal.

Page 191. The title-page of this Bible reads, "The Holy Bible, Conteyning the Old Testament, and the New: Newly translated out of the Original tongues: and with the former Translations diligently compared and revised, by his Majesties speciall Commandment. Appointed to be read in churches." The result, as is well known, of the work of fifty-four pious and learned scholars on the basis of at least some half-dozen earlier versions, this famous book needs no further comment here.

Page 195. Coryate was really a serious traveler, notwithstanding a certain jauntiness in his literary manner and gait, which explains the extraordinary gathering of panegyrical verses in semi-ironical vein which precedes his book.

Page 202. The dedication of Beaumont's only masque to Bacon, who countenanced and financed it, as we should say, offers us an interesting juncture of two such names and a glimpse into the coöperation of the templars in their private entertainment.

Page 203. This witty comedy was given at court on February 27, 1613, but the reference on the title-page to Blackfriars shows that it was originally produced by the Chapel or Revels not later than 1609 and probably before *Byron* in 1608. Chapman's attitude towards the printed play is shown in his justification of his dedication.

Page 204. The epistles prefixed to *A Woman is a Weathercock* are of value; the dedication informing us that the customary dedicatory fee for a play was forty shillings, and the preface, asserting that the stationer insisted on the epistle to the reader, reveals that he was appealing to the public for sales.

Page 206. It is notable that Heywood should have dedicated such a work to his "friends and fellowes the citty-actors"; and his attitude in their defense is a credit to his heart as to his head.

Page 209. No one could better turn an epigram or write a dedication than Ben Jonson; though none could equal him in his contempt and scorn of the base multitude.

Page 211. We have here a deliberate appeal from the hasty judgment of the theatre to the higher court of the reading audience. Webster's certainty of his place among the foremost playwrights of his age speaks forth with confidence in his words.

Page 213. Thomas Shelton was the earliest translator into English of Don Quixote. The translation won immediate popularity, and references to Don Quixote's adventures were soon frequent in English literature. There are almost no facts concerning Shelton's life, and were it not for the information concerning the translation revealed by the dedication, we should not be even thus much enlightened. Shelton reproduces the robust phraseology and spirit of the original and his version is still unsuperseded.

Page 215. Michael Drayton, next to Spenser, was the most popular poet of his day. He could poetize anything as *Poly-olbion,* this famous and patriotic topographical description of England, abundantly proves. The first part of *Poly-olbion* was dedicated to Prince Henry, who gave Drayton a pension of ten pounds for it. In the preface to Part II, "To any that will read it," Drayton criticizes the stationers for omitting the epistle to the reader in Part I where he scolded his readers roundly. Apparently the stationer had more business acumen than the poet.

Page 219. Beaumont's burlesque of the popular citizen's drama in this play was not well taken and the play failed. Hence the author's disavowal in publication of "any intent to wrong anybody," an avowal which we may well accept.

Page 220. "Resolute John Florio" as he signs himself, after several patrons in Elizabeth's reign, became Reader in Italian to Queen Anne and later Gentleman Extraordinary and Groom of the Privy Chamber to the King. His translation of Montaigne, which enjoyed much popularity and afforded Shakespeare material for at least one passage in *The Tempest,* offers an interesting example of the practice of multiple dedication, the three books being dedicated to six noble ladies. Similarly, he renamed his *Italian English Dictionary, Queen Anne's New World of Words* in a new edition in 1611.

Page 222. From this dedication we learn that friends and patrons at times desired manuscript copies of plays, that the author might have difficulty in recovering such a manuscript (presumably from the company) especially if the play had failed. A manuscript of this play is extant, and the relation of some of the songs in *Macbeth* to Middleton's play gives it a peculiar interest.

Page 223. William Browne, delightful pastoralist and lyric poet, wrote this masque, according to custom, for the delight of his fellow members of the Inner Temple.

Page 224. The Countess of Bedford was one of the universal patrons of the age and was fittingly addressed here in behalf of her lately deceased young brother, Lord Harrington, who had perished not without suspicion of foul play.

Page 225. Barnaby Rich, author and soldier, rose to the rank of captain. He served in the low countries with Churchyard and Gascoigne and other adventurers of literary tastes and emulated their example as writers. His pamphlets are curious pictures of the age and vehement invectives against vice in all forms. The deadly sins are denounced each in turn; while lawyers, physicians, landlords, and papists are among his groups of "viperous people." In the epilogue, Rich declares this his twenty-fourth publication.

Page 227. Richard Brathwaite, a gentleman by birth but an inveterate writer, filled as nearly as possible under differing conditions the rôle of a newspaper man. His *Strappado for the Divell* is a characteristic gathering-in of verses of various kinds, mostly satires and epigrams, illustrative of the manners of his age; and their moods—now grim, now playful, rarely cruel—are as varied as their kind.

Page 228. In 1610 George Sandys began his travels in the East; and in 1615 published *A Relation of a Journey begun An. Dom. 1610,* which is descriptive of the Turkish empire, Egypt, the Holy Land, Italy, and the adjoining islands. The government, antiquities, customs of the people, and particularly the religion are faithfully presented. These travels are pleasant to read and they reveal Sandys' erudition and sagacity.

Page 231. George Wither was first a Royalist, then a Puritan. Though flattery meant favor, his spirit was too independent to write adulatory dedications. For his book, *Abuses Stript and Whipt,* Wither was imprisoned in the Marshalsea. During his confinement there, he wrote pastorals, *The Shepherds Hunting,* which he dedicated to his visitants in prison. Some of Wither's best known and most beautiful poetry is found in the fourth eclogue where occurs the classic eulogy on the power of poetry.

Page 236. Lord Burleigh's *Certain Precepts* was printed anonymously after his death and enjoyed, like the other many books of the type, a considerable popularity. It has been surmised that Polonius' famous advice to his sons was a take-off of this sort of thing if not of the sage counselor himself.

Page 238. The title of this book is said to present the earliest printed use of the term New England, a usage confirmed by King Charles who favored the employment of English place names for "barbarous" Indian place names. Smith, who was a great voyager, is most popularly remembered for his story of Pocahontas who visited London and died there. As usual, in the literature of colonization, Smith's pamphlet mingles the exploitation of the natural resources and material advantages of colonization with the missionary spirit which is deeply concerned with the spiritual welfare of the Indians.

Page 239. In the tuneful choir of Elizabethan musicians, Campion stands supreme as the only one of whom we may confidently affirm that he composed both the music and the words. Campion was a physician likewise, and a man of the highest culture.

Page 240. Daniel, noted personally above, had already written history in rhyme in his *Civil Wars*. It was inevitable that he should carry on this popular and somewhat dangerous activity later in prose. *The History of England from the Conquest to the Reign of Edward III* dedicated to Queen Anne was fostered under her patronage.

Page 242. Fines Moryson enjoyed a species of traveling fellowship from the University of Cambridge by the terms of which he traveled widely through Germany, the Low Countries, Switzerland, Italy, Denmark, Poland, and Austria; passing the winters at Leipzig, Leyden, Padua, and Venice; observing minutely and recording industriously the physical aspects of the country, the political organization, national traits, manners, methods of transportation, architecture, food, dress, coinage, and all manner of interesting detail. He first wrote his *Itinerary* in Latin, then translated it into English, and finally wrote a condensed version.

Page 246. This note as to an out-of-the-way drama, not without its humble merit, is interesting as affording corroborative evidence of the dangers which even minor productions suffered of "escaping into print."

Page 247. *A Months Minde,* forming part of the collection of religious verse known as *The Songs of Sion,* has for theme the subject of death. A Biblical verse forms the prelude of each "thought" which is followed by an original song of consolation. In 1618, because of differences with Archbishop Laud, Loe, who was chaplain in ordinary to James I, accepted the pastorate of the English church in Hamburg. He dedicated his verse to different English merchants of Hamburg.

Page 249. George Sandys, the son of a Bishop of York, translated the *Metamorphosis* of Ovid to beguile the tediousness of a sojourn in the colony of Virginia while acting as secretary to the governor there. This was in 1621 when the famous voyage of the *Mayflower* was all but contemporary. Sandys' constant use of the couplet in his translation has been held not to have been without its influence on Dryden and Pope.

Page 251. This epoch-making tragi-comedy, written probably in 1609, appeared in quarto form in 1620 as printed for Thomas Walkley, and again for the same publisher in 1622. In his epistle to the reader, Walkley disavows responsibility for himself or his printer for the corrupted text of his first quarto, and claims credit for reforming the second. *Philaster* was popular both on the stage and in print; two court performances were given in the winter of 1612–13, and five editions were published in nineteen years.

Page 252. *Sheretine and Mariana* is a poem of heroic type, the source of which is "Hungarian history" and the elaborate events of which do not interest us here. It is more to the purpose to recall that the work is dedicated to that universal patron of literature, Lucy, Countess of Bedford.

Page 253. *The Compleat Gentleman,* the work by which Peacham is best known, was written for William Howard, Lord Arundel's youngest son, a boy of eight, to whom it is dedicated. This preface to the reader informs us of the circumstances that inspired it. The details of a nobleman's education are planned. Arts and athletic exercises are encouraged. In his book, Peacham criticizes flogging in schools, strongly recommends travel, and insists on the study of heraldry. The third edition, 1661, presents additional notes on blazonry by Thomas Blount; and it is from this volume that Dr. Johnson drew the heraldic definitions in his dictionary.

Page 256. It is not unfitting to close this collection with the dedication and address to the reader of the most famous book of the age. In these varied addresses to the reader by publisher, printer, procurer, and author, the subscription of the name or initials of any one of these contains no serious claim as to who really wrote the words in question. Obviously neither of Shakespeare's fellows, Heming nor Condell, commanded a style of the grace and ease of this matter prefatory to the first collected edition of Shakespeare's plays. And the similarity of this style to that of Jonson's, even to the employment of certain allusions and illustrations, has not escaped the scrutiny of diligent scholars. What could be more fitting than that the collected work of the greatest dramatist of his age should be ushered to the public by the greatest of his fellow playwrights? Jonson's immortal poem, "To the Memory of my beloved the Author Mr. William Shakespeare and what he hath left us," which is likewise a part of this prefatory material, should make as to this question "assurance doubly sure."

(For the above note especially, I am indebted to Professor Schelling. See his essay, "The Seedpod of Shakespearian Criticism" in *Shakespeare and "Demi-Science,"* pp. 26–48.)

BIBLIOGRAPHY

BIBLIOGRAPHY

Exclusive of the books used in the preparation of the text, the following list is offered with no pretense to completeness.

Adams, Joseph Q. *Life of William Shakespeare.* Boston. New York. Houghton. 1923.

Aikin, Lucy. *Memoirs of the Court of Queen Elizabeth.* London. 1819. 2v.

Albright, Evelyn M. *Dramatic Publication in England, 1580–1640.* Monograph Series, Modern Language Association of America. New York. Heath. London. Oxford University Press. 1927.

—— "Notes on the Status of Literary Property, 1500–45." *Modern Philology.* (1919), XVII, 439–55.

—— "To Be Staied." *Publications of the Modern Language Association.* (1915), XXX, 474 ff.

Ames, Joseph. *Typographical Antiquities.* "Being an historical account of printing in England, with some memoirs of . . . printers and a register of books. . . . (1471–1600)." London. W. Faden. 1749.

Arber, Edward. Editor of *An English Garner.* London. 1877–97.

—— *English Reprints.* London. 1869——. 30v.

—— *English Scholars' Library.* London. 1878–84. 16v.

—— Stationers' Registers, *see* London. Stationers' Company.

Aubrey, John. *Brief Lives.* Edited by Andrew Clark. 1898.

Beljame, Alexandre. *Le public et les hommes de lettres en Angleterre au dix-huitième siècle. 1660–1744.* Paris. 1897.

Bibliographical Society of London. *Transactions.*

Library (indexed here according to authors).

Birch, Thomas. *Memoirs of the Reign of Queen Elizabeth,* "from the year 1581 till her death." London. 1754. 2v.

—— *The Life of Henry Prince of Wales.* Dublin. 1760.

Bodleian Library (Oxford). *Catalogue of Printed Books and Manuscripts.*

Bourne, H. R. Fox. *Sir Philip Sidney*. London. New York. 1891.

British Museum. *Catalogue of Books in the Library of the British Museum Printed in England, Scotland, and Ireland, and of Books in English Printed Abroad to the Year 1640*. Compiled by A. H. Bullen. 1884. 3v.

—— *Catalogue of Harleian Manuscripts in the British Museum.* London. G. Eyre and A. Strahan. 1808–12.

—— *Catalogue of Lansdowne Manuscripts in the British Museum;* with indexes. London. R. and A. Taylor. 1819.

Brooke, C. F. Tucker. *Shakespeare of Stratford.* New Haven. Yale University Press. 1926.

Brown, W. F. Wyndham. "The Origin and Growth of Copyright." *Law Magazine and Review*. (1909), 54–65.

Cambridge History of English Literature. Edited by A. W. Ward and A. R. Waller. Cambridge University Press. 1909–10. Vols. III, IV, V, VI.

Chambers, Sir Edmund K. *The Elizabethan Stage.* London. Oxford University Press. 1923. 4v.

Cheyney, Edward P. *A History of England from the Defeat of the Armada to the Death of Elizabeth*. New York. 1914–26. 2v.

Collier, John P. *A Bibliographical and Critical Account of the Rarest Books in the English Language*. London. 1865. 2v.

Collins, A. S. *Authorship in the Days of Johnson*. "Being a study of the relation between author, patron, publisher, and the public between 1726–1780." London. 1927.

Conley, C. H. *The First English Translators of the Classics*. New Haven. Yale University Press. 1927.

Creizenach, Wilhelm. *Geschichte des Neueren Dramas.* Halle. 1911.

—— *English Drama in the Age of Shakespeare*. Translated from *Geschichte des Neueren Dramas*. London. Philadelphia. 1916.

Day, Angell. *The English Secretorie,* "or method of writing of epistles and letters." London. 1635.

Dibdin, Thomas F. *Typographical Antiquities . . .*, 1471–1600 . . . "begun by . . . Joseph Ames, considerably augmented by William Herbert, and now greatly enlarged, with copious notes, . . ." London. W. Miller. 1810–19. 4v.

Dictionary of National Biography. Edited by Leslie Stephen and Sir Sidney Lee. London. Oxford University Press. 1930.

D'Israeli, Isaac. *Amenities of Literature*. London. 1859. 2v.

Duff, Edward Gordon. *A Century of the English Book Trade, 1457–1557*. London. Bibliographical Society. 1905.

—— *Early Printed Books*. London. 1893.

Ellis, Sir Henry. *Original Letters of Eminent Literary Men of the 16th., 17th., and 18th. Centuries*. London. For the Camden Society. J. B. Nichols. 1843.

Esdaile, Arundel. *A Student's Manual of Bibliography*. London. The Library Association. 1931.

Fowell, Frank, and Frank Palmer. *Censorship in England*. London. Frank Palmer. 1913.

Gildersleeve, Virginia. *Government Regulation of the Elizabethan Drama*. New York. Columbia University Studies in English (1908). Ser. II, Vol. IV, No. I.

Gray, W. Forbes. *The Poets Laureate of England*. London. 1914.

Greg, Walter W. "An Elizabethan Printer and His Copy." *Bibliographical Society Transactions*. (1923), 102–118.

—— "Prompt Copies, Private Transcripts, and the Playhouse Scrivener." *Library*. (1925–26), 148–156.

—— *The First Folio and Its Publishers*. London. Shakespeare Association. 1924.

—— "Tottel's Miscellany." *Library*. (1904), 113–133.

—— Editor of *Henslowe's Diary*. London. 1904–1908. 2v.

Grolier Club, New York. *Catalogue of Original and Early Editions of Some of the Poetical and Prose Works of English Writers from Langland to Wither* . . . "being a contribution to the bibliography of English literature." New York. For the Grolier Club. 1905.

Harleian Miscellany. "A collection of scarce, curious, and entertaining pamphlets and tracts." London. 1808–11. 12v.

Harrison, George B. *An Elizabethan Journal. 1591–1594*. New York. 1929.

—— *A Second Elizabethan Journal. 1595–1598*. London. 1931.

—— "Books and Readers." *Library*. (1927–28), 273–302.

Hazlitt, William C. *Hand-book* "to the popular, poetical, and dramatic literature of Great Britain from the invention of printing to the Restoration." London. 1867. Continued by his *Collections and Notes.* London. 1876–1903. 6v.

—— *Prefaces, Dedications, and Epistles Selected from Early Books. 1540–1701.* London. Privately printed. 1874.

Holzknecht, Karl. *Literary Patronage in the Middle Ages.* Philadelphia. University of Pennsylvania. 1923.

Laing, David. Editor of *Notes of Ben Jonson's Conversations with William Drummond of Hawthornden.* London. Shakespeare Society. (1842), Vol. IX.

Lang, Andrew. *Social England Illustrated.* "A collection of 17th century tracts." In Arber, *English Garner.* Westminster. 1903.

Lee, Sir Sidney. "An Elizabethan Bookseller." *Bibliographica.* London. (1895), 474–498.

—— *A Life of William Shakespeare.* New York. 1927.

—— *Bibliographical History of the First Folio.* London. 1905.

—— Facsimile of the First Folio edition of Shakespeare's Plays, 1623. Oxford. Clarendon Press. 1902.

—— *Great Englishmen of the Sixteenth Century.* London. 1904.

London. Stationers' Company. *A Transcript of the Registers of the Company of Stationers of London. 1554–1640.* Edited by Edward Arber. Birmingham. Privately printed. 1875–94. 5v. with index.

Lowndes, William Thomas. *The Bibliographer's Manual of English Literature.* London. H. G. Bohn. 1883–1885. 6v.

McKerrow, Ronald B. *A Dictionary of Printers and Booksellers in England, Scotland, and Ireland, and of Foreign Printers of English Books, 1557–1640.* London. Bibliographical Society. 1910.

—— *An Introduction to Bibliography for Literary Students.* Oxford. Clarendon Press. 1927.

—— "Booksellers, Printers, and Stationers' Trade . . ." In *Shakespeare's England.* London. Oxford University Press. 1916. Vol. II, Ch. XXII.

—— "Edward Alde as a Typical Trade Printer." *Library.* (1929–30), 121–162.

—— "Richard Robinson's *Eupolemia, Archippus, and Panoplia.*" 1603. (A ms. containing an account of his literary earnings.) *Gentleman's Magazine* (April 1906), 277–284.

Madan, Falconer. "Early Representations of the Printing Press." *Bibliographica.* London. (1895–97), I, 223–249.

Moore, Samuel. "General Aspects of Literary Patronage in the Middle Ages." *Library.* (1913), 369–392.

—— "Patrons of Letters in Norfolk and Suffolk *c.* 1450." *Publications of the Modern Language Association.* (1912–13), XXVII–XXVIII.

Nichols, John. *The Progresses and Public Processions of Queen Elizabeth.* London. 1823. 3v.

Onions, Charles T. Editor of *Shakespeare's England.* London. Oxford University Press. 1916. 2v.

Penniman, Josiah H. *The War of the Theatres.* University of Pennsylvania Series in Philology, Literature, and Archæology. Boston. (1897), Vol. IV. No. III.

Plomer, Henry R. "Henry Bynneman, Printer, 1566–1583." *Library.* (1908), 225–244.

—— *Short History of English Printing, 1476–1898.* London. 1900.

—— "The Printers of Shakespeare's Plays and Poems." *Library.* (1906), 149–167.

—— "Thomas East, Printer." *Library.* (1901), 298–310.

—— "Two Law-Suits of Richard Pynson." *Library.* (1909), 115–151.

Pollard, Alfred W. "Authors, Players, and Pirates in Shakespeare's Day." *Library.* (1916), 73–101.

—— "Regulation of the Book Trade in the Sixteenth Century." *Library.* (1916), 18–43.

—— *Shakespeare's Fight with the Pirates and the Problems of the Transmission of His Text.* London. A. Moring. 1917.

—— *Shakespeare Folios and Quartos.* "A Study in the Bibliography of Shakespeare's Plays, 1594–1685." London. F. Methuen. 1909.

—— and G. Redgrave. Compilers of *A Short-Title Catalogue* "of books printed in England, Scotland, and Ireland, and of English books printed abroad, 1475–1640." London. 1926.

Putnam, George Haven. *Books and Their Makers During the Middle Ages.*

London and New York. 1896–1897. 2v. (Vol. I: 476–1600) (Vol. II: 1500–1709.)

Rhodes, R. Crompton. *Shakespeare's First Folio.* Oxford. 1923.

Rimbault, Edward Francis. *Bibliotheca Madrigaliana.* London. 1847.

Rymer, Thomas, and Robert Sanderson, editors. *Fœdera, Conventiones, Literae, et . . . Acta Publica (1101–1726). Syllabus of Rymer's Fœdera in English,* by Sir Thomas D. Hardy. London. 1873. 3v.

Schelling, Felix E. *Elizabethan Drama, 1558–1642.* Boston. New York. 1908. 2v.

——*English Literature During the Lifetime of Shakespeare.* New York. 1928.

——*Shakespeare and "Demi-Science."* Philadelphia. University of Pennsylvania Press. 1927.

Shaaber, Matthias A. *Some Forerunners of the Newspaper in England 1476–1622.* Philadelphia. University of Pennsylvania Press. 1929.

Sheavyn, Phoebe. *The Literary Profession in the Elizabethan Age.* Manchester University Press. 1909.

Shipherd, Henry Robinson. "Play Publishing in Elizabethan Times." *Publications of the Modern Language Association,* (1919), XXXIV, 590–600.

Smith, George Gregory. *Elizabethan Critical Essays.* Oxford. Clarendon Press. 1904. 2v.

Smith, Preserved. *A History of Modern Culture.* Vol. I: 1543–1687. New York. 1930. 2v.

Spingarn, J. E. *Critical Essays of the Seventeenth Century.* Vol. I: 1605–1650. Oxford. Clarendon Press. 1908.

State Papers, Domestic. *Calendar of State Papers, Domestic Series,* of the reigns of Elizabeth and James I preserved in the Public Record Office (1547–1625). Edited by R. Lemon and M. A. E. Green. London. 1856–1872.

Stationers' Company. *See* London. Stationers' Company.

Strickland, Agnes. *Lives of the Queens of England.* London. G. Bell. 1888–1891. Vol. III.

Symonds, John Addington (the younger). *Sir Philip Sidney.* London. 1885.

Timperley, Charles H. *Dictionary of Printers and Printing . . . Ancient and Modern . . . to 1838*. London. H. Johnson. 1839.

Venn, John, and J. A. Venn. Compilers of *Alumni Cantabrigienses*. "A biographical list of all known students, at the University of Cambridge, from the earliest times to 1900." Cambridge University Press. 1922.

Wheatley, H. B. *The Dedication of Books to Patron and Friend*. London. 1887.

Wilson, John Dover. *The Copy for 'Hamlet,' 1603, and the 'Hamlet' Transcript, 1593*. London. A. Moring. 1918.

—— and Alfred W. Pollard. "How Some of Shakespeare's Plays Were Pirated." *London Times Literary Supplement*. (Jan. 17, 1919), p. 30.

Wood, Anthony à. *Athenæ Oxonienses*. "An exact history of all the writers and bishops, who have had their education in the University of Oxford, from . . . 1500 to the end of the year 1690. . . ." London. 1813–20. 4v.

Young, F. C. B. *Mary Sidney, Countess of Pembroke*. London. Nutt. 1912.

INDEX

INDEX OF AUTHORS AND EPISTLES

Chronologically Arranged

www.ingramcontent.com/pod-product-compliance
Lightning Source LLC
Chambersburg PA
CBHW070545310726
48982CB00004B/839
9781512811766